Ruth & Esther

Ruth & Esther

Women in Alien Lands

Johanna
W. H. van Wijk-Bos

ABINGDON PRESS / Nashville

RUTH AND ESTHER
WOMEN IN ALIEN LANDS

by Johanna W.H.van Wijk-Bos

This book is printed on recycled, acid-free paper.

Scripture quotations, unless otherwise indicated, are the author's own translation.

Library of Congress Cataloging-in-Publication Data

Van Wijk-Bos, Johanna W.H., 1940-
Ruth & Esther : women in alien lands / Johanna W. H. van Wijk-Bos.
p. cm.
Includes bibliographical references.
ISBN 0-687-09053-9 (alk. paper)
1. Bible. O.T. Ruth—Criticism, interpretation, etc. 2. Bible. O.T. Esther—Criticism, interpretation, etc. I. Title: Ruth and Esther. II. Title.

BS1315.52 .V36 2001
222'.3507'7—dc21

00-065001

01 02 03 04 05 06 07 08 09 10—10 9 8 7 6 5 4 3 2 1

MANUFACTURED IN THE UNITED STATES OF AMERICA

CONTENTS

INTRODUCTION

Women and the Bible

IF WE HAD TO DRAW UP A LIST OF TEN BIBLICAL WOMEN WHO ARE familiar to us, Ruth and Esther would likely be on it. We might be able to provide a rough outline of their stories, even if some of the details remain a little hazy. Yet, we may not know Ruth and Esther as well as we think. The Book of Ruth may be lodged in our mind as a "peaceful" or "romantic" tale, for example. Of Esther's story we may recall Haman and Mordecai more sharply than Esther herself.

Our partial ignorance arises to a great extent from a lack of attention given to these books in a Christian context of study and devotion. For a long time Ruth and Esther remained virtually unexplored by scholars and congregational leaders. Both of these books deserve to be better known as a part of Christian biblical heritage for a number of reasons: They have women as the central characters and are named after these women, a unique feature among books in the Bible; each book presents a distinctive narrative full of interesting twists and turns; finally, each story portrays features that exemplify the life of biblical faith.

It is especially important to study Ruth and Esther anew in view of the fact that the central characters are women. When we look back to our biblical heritage, it is not easy to find a strong presence of women; and the roots for the roles of women in the church and the life of faith are not clearly discernible. It is of vital importance, then, to retrieve those elements of the biblical story in which women played a major role.

As we begin this study, I invite us to think of ourselves as travelers to a place where we have been before but wish to get to know better. The landscape is familiar—but there are new features in it, and old facets take on new and unexpected forms. As we wander around and pay close attention, vistas may open up that lead us to see the landscape in a different way, to discover places of interest and beauty we had not known existed in this place.

Ruth and Esther play crucial roles, not only within the confines of their own story but within the larger history of God's covenant people, ancient Israel. Thus, these accounts have bearing on God's dealings with the world. Within the Old Testament accounts, Ruth is an important link in the ancestral line that produced David, who became the model for the ideal king. For the Christian world, Ruth is one of the ancestors in the list that leads to Jesus the Christ, as she is mentioned in the Gospel According to Luke (Luke 1:5). Esther appears at a moment in the history of ancient Israel when its very survival is at stake. Both women act within an alien environment. Ruth is a Moabite woman in Judah; Esther is a Jewish woman in Persia. The title of this book means to reflect this reality. They are women in alien lands.

By calling Ruth and Esther women in alien lands, I also intend to point to a deeper reality than just the physical environment. In the Bible, the landscape of the work of redemption is for the most part populated by men. These men are called by God to accomplish the gigantic tasks demanded of them. Ruth and Esther are, as women, not "native" participants in the work of redemption. One could say that they are viewed as "aliens" to the tasks they perform. The alien quality of their environment serves to underline this fact.

In the days of Ruth and Esther women were vulnerable if they did not have a male to protect them. Esther as an orphan and Ruth as a widow belong to a category of women who lack the presence of a male to guarantee their social, economic, and psychological survival. In the case of these two women this reality is aggravated by their foreign status. In the laws of ancient Israel as well as in narrative and prophetic texts, foreigners or strangers, together with orphans and widows, are assigned protected status, a testimony to the fragile nature of their existence (Jeremiah 7:5-7); God is said to be especially interested in their welfare (Exodus 22:21-24); and the people are commanded in multiple ways to look after them (Exodus 23:9; Deuteronomy 10:17-19). Ruth's and Esther's achievements appear all the more remarkable in view of the fact that they each fit two of the three categories.

Today, at least in Western industrialized societies and religious communities, women have greater freedom to exercise choices over their role and function in their communities than did Ruth and Esther. Yet, in some ways and in some parts of the world to a much more severe extent than in others, women's lives today are still limited and vulnerable. In exploring our freedom as well as our limitations and vulnerability, we may find strong connections with Ruth and Esther.

There will be in some respects an alien quality to the nature of the activities of these two women. Esther may appear too submissive on the one hand and too bloodthirsty on the other. Ruth is almost too good to be true, an "ideal" woman that we cannot hope to emulate. It may be helpful not to set up Ruth and Esther as "models" to follow. Rather than seeing them as models, we may try to understand them in their own context, at the same time looking to understand our own lives in our context. Thus, we may learn where our stories and their stories connect—and also where they disconnect. Through this encounter there may come a deeper understanding of the text and of ourselves and our place in God's work of redemption of the creation.

For Reflection and Discussion

1. Of the 1,315 names that occur in the Bible, only 9 percent, 111, are women. What does this figure signify to you? Think of contemporary contexts in which women are equally under-represented or invisible. Give concrete examples. Clip newspaper and magazine features that exhibit this aspect of women's lives.

2. List all the women you know from the Bible. When you have recollected as many as you can, give some specifics for each name. How many names are missing? What does the missing number signify?

3. On March 8, 2000, UNICEF declared a global campaign on violence against women with a focus on acts like "honor killings," dowry deaths, female infanticide, and acid attacks. Are you familiar with this type of violence? Why is it sometimes called "culturally sanctioned gynocide"? Where in the world do these activities take place? Can you think of other culturally sanctioned violence against women? Give specific examples. What about violence against women in the U.S.?

4. From a contemporary context give examples of ways in which women's lives are vulnerable and limited socially, economically, and psychologically. Describe your own experience and how it reflects the same or similar difficulties.

Prayer

God of our past, we give thanks for the great treasure you saved for us in the stories, the laws, and the songs of the Bible. We thank you for the people who lived their lives in your presence, who struggled with the tasks set before them. We are especially grateful for the strong and faithful women that went before us, women who lived lives of strong faith and commitment to you and their neighbor. Teach us to observe their presence and listen to their voices patiently and humbly so that actions and words of the past take on new meaning for us in our lives. Amen.

PART 1
THE BOOK OF RUTH

INTRODUCTION

Date and Context

THE BIBLE IS NOT A HISTORY BOOK, BUT THE TEXTS OF THE BIBLE CAME out of particular historical settings and need to be understood in these settings. The history of the people that produced the Old Testament, or Hebrew Bible, is long and complex; but we need to know a few things if we want to understand the text better. Roughly we may place the texts of the Old Testament between 1200 and 200 B.C. (see "History and the Bible" at the end of the chapter). Unfortunately, there is not much agreement as to the time period in which Ruth was written; some have assigned it to the period of Ezra and Nehemiah (late fifth to fourth centuries B.C.). Others propose as early a date as the ninth century B.C., shortly after the reign of David. Yet others place the origin of the book in the first quarter of the sixth century B.C., shortly before and after the events of the Babylonian Exile. The historical setting of the origin of Ruth is not a problem that can be easily solved.

Let us briefly look at each of these possible settings. If the story of Ruth was first told and written during the reign of Solomon, this would have been a time of relative stability and prosperity. In the absence of crisis, choices between good and evil may be more ambiguous; and people may wonder what exactly constitutes a faithful life and how the presence of God is experienced and made manifest. The book might also serve as a reminder of the existence of vulnerable and fragile groups even in times of prosperity and stability and the need to provide protection for such people. Finally, the story of Ruth provides an ancestral line for David,

Solomon's father. This line goes all the way back to Judah, the son of Jacob and Leah, and Tamar, his daughter-in-law (Ruth 4:18-22; Genesis 38).

If the writing of Ruth took place shortly before and after the Babylonian Exile, the setting would be one of extreme contrast to the first one I proposed. The Exile of the sixth century for the people of Judah brought chaos, disaster, disenfranchisement, doubt, political domination, and religious uncertainty. The background of Ruth is also full of instability: Famine and death are prominent at the opening of the story and stalk the two women, Ruth and Naomi, throughout the narrative until they finally disappear from the scene in the final chapter. There are then direct connections between the lives of the people in the story and the lives of the people who formed the immediate audience. In addition, Ruth walks a sure path of faithfulness under extremely difficult circumstances. She walks this path as a foreigner; thus she is constantly referred to as the Moabite in the story. The story can then be understood to speak of adverse circumstances and ways to live faithfully within such circumstances.

If Ruth was written in the time of the so-called Restoration under Ezra and Nehemiah, it too was a period of anxiety and vulnerability for the community in Judah that was attempting to rebuild itself out of rubble. Ruth may then speak directly to issues of identity for the community of faith. The one who is most faithful is not necessarily an Israelite in this story; the one who is accepted into the family of ancient Israel, the covenant people, is a female foreigner, a precarious position to be in at the time of Ezra and Nehemiah (Ezra 9 and 10; Nehemiah 13:23-27). The book could then be intended as a corrective toward exclusive practices that established the people's identity at the cost of maltreatment of the stranger.

Historical dates assigned to biblical texts often remain in the realm of an educated guess. Since we cannot rule out with certainty any of the time periods here described for Ruth, we will keep the possibilities of all three of these contexts in mind as we explore Ruth. Thus, we can let the different questions and observations as they arise from each period as well as our own questions and observations interact with one another in order to arrive at a deeper understanding of the text.

In the Christian community we are accustomed to finding Ruth in the historical section of the Bible, between Judges and First Samuel. This location goes back to ancient Greek and Latin versions of the Old Testament. In the Hebrew version, Ruth is placed differently, following Proverbs and before the Song of Solomon, both of which are found in the latter third of the Bible, following the Prophets. Ruth is read during the Jewish festival called the Feast of Weeks (Leviticus 23:15-16), at which time the first harvest of the year in springtime is celebrated.

Redemption: A Social Practice and Religious Concept

One of the central theological concepts in Ruth is that of redemption. Redemption was a practice and idea that lived both in the social and religious realm in ancient Israel. First, redemption pointed to the responsibility people had for one another. Redeemers were people in the ancient Israelite society who were appointed to take care of those who could not take care of themselves. Various redemption customs existed in ancient Israel in regard to property, the safeguarding of individual freedom, and vengeance (Leviticus 25–27; Numbers 35:19). Individuals executing redemption responsibilities were always males, since women did not have the necessary legal rights to act in this capacity.

Although only males could take on the function of a redeemer in a social context and the term *redeemer* is not used for Ruth herself, Ruth, in fact, is portrayed as one who acts in the capacity of a redeemer toward Naomi. She makes herself responsible for Naomi's loneliness (1:16-17), for her welfare (2:2, 18; 3:17), and for her lack of children (4:14 and following).

Ancient Israel applied the idea of redemption also to God. God was held responsible for the welfare of the people. Thus, God could be called to account when things were not going well in the life of the community or the individual. Naomi's complaint against God in Chapter 1 (1:21) testifies to this notion.

It may be a new idea for us to think of redemption as something that functioned first of all in the human community. For Christians, the word *redemption* has a particular set of religious connotations and functions almost solely in the world of religious convictions. The Book of Ruth provides an opportunity to expand our understanding of this word, as the story shows the extent of the practice and its function in the human community as well as its connection to the life of faith.

The Form of the Story

Each chapter of the book forms a distinct unit with Chapters 1 and 4 shaping a type of framework around the inner chapters, 2 and 3. The problems that arise in Chapter 1 are resolved in Chapter 4. In the opening of the story a family leaves its place of origin, Bethlehem (1:1), which in the final episodes is in the center (4:1-12). People disappear from view in the first episode until only Ruth and Naomi are left (1:1-14); in Chapter 4 the community populates the scene, both at the city gate and around Naomi (4:1-17). The death of the family members in the first verses of Chapter 1 is balanced and in some sense resolved by the fruitful marriage of Ruth and Boaz (4:13). The neighbor women receive sharp words from Naomi at the end of Chapter 1 (1:19-21), and in the last chapter Naomi receives words of love and praise from them (4:15-17).

Chapters 2 and 3 both show Ruth and Boaz at the center (2:3-16 and 3:6-15) with a conversation between Naomi and Ruth at the opening and conclusion of the chapters (2:1-2, 17-22 and 3:1-5, 16-18). The roles of the characters show development and some contrast. Ruth opens the conversation with Naomi in Chapter 2, to which Naomi responds briefly (2:2); but Naomi opens in Chapter 3 with the outlines of a plan and directives for Ruth (3:1-4). Boaz takes the initiative when encountering Ruth in the field (2:8 and following), but on the threshing floor Ruth makes a daring countermove by pointing out to Boaz what his duties are (3:9). In Chapter 2 all the actions take place by the light of day in public (2:3-17). Chapter 3 depicts the important action in the dark, at a place hidden from view (3:6-15).

Certain words and phrases are woven through the story to give it coherence and to emphasize major motifs. Words that recur in a text, sometimes with different shades of meaning, are called "keywords." Hebrew storytelling used keywords to great effect. In my translation I have always rendered a Hebrew word with the same English equivalent in order not to lose the importance of certain motifs in the story. Hebrew is flexible in terms of word order in a sentence and can vary word order for emphasis. I follow the Hebrew order as much as possible in the English translation so that we keep some of the flavor of the Hebrew sentence.

For Reflection and Discussion

All of us live in a time far removed from the centuries during which the texts of the Bible were written and collected, and most of us live in a place that is equally removed. To understand a story or a book one needs some familiarity with the circumstances and the place that produced the material. To make things more complicated, the part of the Bible called the Old Testament by Christians, the Tanakh of the Jews, was written over a period of about one thousand years. There is a lot of background material available on the history of ancient Israel, its social and economic life, the development of its religion, and the lives of women. This book contains a list of resources on these subjects, to which I refer those who would like to know more detail. Here I provide a brief overview of the main events in the history of the people who created the texts of the Old Testament/Hebrew Bible and for whom these texts were written.

History and the Bible

Remember to count "backward" when it concerns a period B.C. (Before Christ):

1200–200: The time in which the books of the Bible of the Old Testament/Hebrew Bible were written and collected.

1200–1000: A league of tribes lived in Palestine, who later became the people I call ancient Israel. In the Bible they are usually called "the children of Israel," or "Israel," or "Israel and Judah." The designation "Hebrew" for the people is rather rare in the Old Testament and is reserved for special usage. The language of the people and therefore of the Old Testament/Hebrew Bible is Hebrew with some small sections written in Aramaic (which became the spoken and written language of the people sometime after the Babylonian Exile). A word that is translated with the English word *Jew* begins to occur toward the last part of the period in which the Hebrew Bible originated, after the fifth century B.C.; and it comes from the association of the people with the province of Judah. In Hebrew the word is literally *Judahite*. You will find this designation in the biblical books of Ezra, Nehemiah, Esther, and Daniel.

1000–933: The first formation of the monarchy, first under the military command of Saul and then under David and Solomon. This was a period of increased stability with the threat of the Philistines finally put to rest by David and with major building projects as well as expansion of territory undertaken by Solomon. The one kingdom lasted only for a period of two kings. One theory places the origin of Ruth at this time.

933–720: Two kingdoms. One in the northern part of the country, in the Bible, confusingly, also called "Israel." One in the southern part, including Jerusalem, called in the Bible "Judah." With brief exceptions there were few stable periods in these two centuries, and the kingdoms were beset by hostilities from outside and from one another.

720–587: The kingdom of Judah. In 720, the Northern Kingdom fell to Assyria, which took the majority of the population into exile and repopulated the cities. A group in the New Testament called the Samaritans go back to a mix of the Israelite population and the imported populations of this area. From 720 until 587, there was only one very small kingdom: Judah. This tiny entity had little political independence, although it endured for another 135 years. Finally, it succumbed to the threat of Babylonia, the empire that had conquered Assyria in Mesopotamia.

587–538: Babylonian Conquest and Exile. This period is of great significance for understanding the Bible. The city of Jerusalem was conquered, the Temple was destroyed, and a large part of the people were deported to Babylonia. These events brought destabilization of life in all its forms. Politically, socially, and economically the people were devastated. Moreover, the people in Judah had held the land as a result of what they believed to be a promise by God. They understood themselves to be in a special relationship with God, in a covenant that could not be broken. They viewed their God as the most powerful of all the gods that existed and One who would conquer the enemy in a show of strength. These beliefs and hopes were defeated during the Conquest and Exile; and they needed to rebuild themselves, their city, and their identity as well as their central beliefs during the period after the Exile. Some scholars place Ruth in this context.

538–333: The period of the Restoration. This period concerns the province of Judah, mainly the city of Jerusalem, after Cyrus of Persia (the empire that conquered Babylonia) issued an edict in 538 that allowed the exiles from Judah to return home. He provided them with resources to reconstruct their existence. The leaders Ezra and Nehemiah were active at some time during this period and provided crucial guidance in reconstruction of the city and the Temple. In addition, there was an emphasis on gathering and codifying texts that later were to make up the Hebrew Bible. This period is marked by a struggle for identity and, in certain quarters, resistance to outside influence that could be seen as threatening to the survival of the small group. Ruth may have its origins in this setting and sound a note of disapproval to those who would draw the lines around the community too tightly and who were too certain of who belonged and who was outside.

Not everyone who could go home to Judah did go home. From this time on, we may date the beginnings of the Jewish Dispersion or Diaspora, which refers to substantial communities of Jews who lived in the midst of empires where they were aliens.

Life in the Diaspora continues and flourishes.

333–63: Greek domination. This period was marked by the threat of assimilation because of the pressure of Greek culture. Such threats are portrayed in the Book of Daniel, for example. Esther reflects tensions from this period also but more from the perspective of those living in the Dispersion.

Read the Book of Ruth all the way through. Do this a couple of times to get significant detail into view.

Questions

1. How large an area do you envision the land of David and Solomon to be? How many people lived there? What type of society existed? (Agricultural, nomadic, rural, urban, and so forth). What about the time after the Babylonian Exile?

2. Can you identify some prophets and place them in their proper historical period? What concerns of the prophets do you see reflected in Ruth?

3. I use the word *story* for Ruth. Is this book also history? In what sense is it different from contemporary history, if we consider the book historical?

Prayer

God of our lives, we thank you for the glimpses we have of you in the lives of those who went before us, who walked their path with you in glad obedience. May we consider their wisdom and grace and learn from them. God of history, story, and song, enliven our imagination that we may hear old stories with new ears and see them with new eyes. Make us eager for new teaching, and may our view of the past make us hopeful for the future. Amen.

Chapter 1
A Woman's Complaint
(Ruth 1)

THE FIRST CHAPTER CAN BE DIVIDED INTO THREE SECTONS. THE FIRST SIX verses serve to set the scene of a family of emigrants from Bethlehem living in Moab because of famine, the death of its male members, and the decision of the remaining female Bethlehemite to return home. The introduction also serves to draw the woman, Naomi, into focus. The time-flow is fast in the opening sentences, and years have gone by before Naomi makes her decision to go back home. In the middle section, verses 7-18, time is at a standstill as Naomi argues with her daughters-in-law, who have accompanied her for a part of the trip, to go back to their own homes. In the end, after some strenuous persuading, Orpah agrees; but Ruth stays with her mother-in-law. The spotlight is on Naomi and Ruth in this episode. Naomi is of the opinion that only male presence in their lives can save them from complete disaster. Ruth refuses to leave Naomi and joins herself to her mother-in-law as closely and formally as she can. The last episode (verses 19-22) pictures the two women on their arrival in Bethlehem. Only Naomi speaks, and her utterance does not acknowledge Ruth's companionship or its value. The chapter ends on a note of hope, however, so the listener's expectations are raised for what is to follow. The story is told with elegance and skill, leaving the audience to draw its conclusions by inference and wordplay.

Judahites in Moab
Ruth 1:1-6

1. Once, in the days that the judges judged, there was a famine in the land, and a man from Bethlehem, Judah, went to live as a stranger in the domain of Moab, he and his woman and his two sons. 2. The name of the man was Elimelech, and the name of his woman Naomi, and the name of their two sons Mahlon and Chilion;—Ephrathites from Bethlehem, Judah—they arrived at the Moab domain and were there. 3. Then died Elimelech, the man of Naomi and she was left behind, she and her two sons. 4. They took for themselves women of Moab, the name of the one Orpah, and the name of the second Ruth; and they lived there for ten years. 5. Then died also the two of them, Mahlon and Chilion, and she was left behind, the woman, without her two children and her man.

6. And she arose, she and her daughters-in-law, and she returned from the domain of Moab for she heard in the domain of Moab that the Holy One visited his people by giving them bread.

The first six verses provide the introduction to the book and serve also to set the stage for what is to follow immediately. The story begins simply, but a great deal is told in a few words. The opening words, *in the days that the judges judged,* place the events to be told in a particular period of ancient Israel's history before the tribes had coalesced into a kind of unity and while there was recurring hostility from outside. The period is familiar to us from the Book of Judges in the Bible, and the accounts there are full of turmoil and distress. The last chapters of Judges especially convey painful and chaotic episodes (Judges 19–21). These incidents are introduced as well as concluded by the observation that "there was no king in Israel" (Judges 19:1 and 21:25). The last words of the entire Book of Judges are "all the people did what was right in their own eyes" (Judges 21:25). In Christian Bibles Ruth follows directly on Judges, and the opening phrase of Ruth may draw our attention to a setting posed by the biblical text as one in which pretty much anything could happen. There was after all no king, and the implication is that this absence makes for an unstable situation. The opening of Ruth also paves the way for its ending, which provides an ancestral list for David. The last word in Ruth is *David* (4:22). David was not just any king; he was the one with whom God entered into a special covenant. He became the model for the ideal king. The story of Ruth by its opening and closing words is placed in a time of potential chaos and disaster but looks forward to a time of harmony and societal well-being.

In addition to providing a time period, the narrator informs the listeners that there was a *famine in the land.* Famines are mentioned in the Bible frequently because they were regular and devastating occurrences in an area where rainfall was irregular and undependable. Because starvation and disease go hand in hand with famines, social and economic upheaval are familiar side effects. The story of Ruth thus places itself emphatically in uncertain times when instability of the social and political structures were the order of the day and when communal and individual survival was threatened.

Famines are not a familiar phenomenon today in the industrialized sector of the northern hemisphere, but they are certainly a reality in a great part of the world that we know. Global problems are brought to everyone's attention daily; so all of us, whether through the news or through intimate acquaintance, know something of the horror of famine. In such times, families may pack up and leave home and country to try and make it in a place with better chances for survival. Elimelech from Bethlehem did just this; he took his family and went to live in Moab, the country directly to the east of Bethlehem on the other side of the Dead Sea. The frequent mention of Moab in the first six verses (five times) raises awareness of the fact that Elimelech and Naomi's family were aliens and that they lived in a land that was perceived as hostile and perverse (Genesis 19:30-38; Numbers 25:1-3; Deuteronomy 23:3-4; Jeremiah 48; Amos 2:1-3). The phrase *to live as a stranger* indicates the fragility of the life they substituted for the threat of starvation in Bethlehem. The life of the stranger in the cultures of the ancient Near East was beset by difficulty. These folk led uncomfortable lives on the margin of the groups where they sojourned without the rights and privileges of those who belonged. This mention of life as a stranger in a hostile place is the third factor that alerts the astute reader to the dangerous realities that are and will be the context for this story.

Then, the males of this family that fled death in its native land all die in their adopted country. First comes the announcement of the death of Elimelech. This negative note is compensated for by the mention of the sons' marriages; but soon these two died also, and Naomi *was left behind, the woman, without her two children and her man.* Twice the introduction mentions that Naomi was *left behind* (verses 3 and 5), the second time referring to her not by name but as *the woman*, a word choice that underlines her vulnerability. Male presence has left the life of Naomi, and the words *left behind* have an ominous ring. In such circumstances there was little hope for survival. The presence of her daughters-in-law did not count as an alleviation of her precarious situation and could in fact aggravate the seriousness of her predicament. Only by inference can we tell the marriages of the two sons have not produced offspring, even though ten years have gone by. There is an implication, at least, of barrenness in the case of Orpah and Ruth, which is significant for the rest of the story; for it casts doubt on Ruth's capacity to have children.

Absence of children, especially male children, spelled disaster for the future. The storyteller has introduced a family, removed all the males (that is life-support) from the stage, and in so doing focused all attention on the ones that are *left behind*. The spotlight is now on three women, three childless widows. The story began in a fast tempo and let a relatively long time flow by in six verses. The tempo of the story will alternate from fast in descriptive parts to slow in vital moments of decision. Such a decisive moment is about to take place.

Verse 6 serves as both the closing of the introduction and the opening of the next episode. For the first time in the tale Naomi is in charge, *and she arose, . . . and she returned. . . .* One of the keywords of the first chapter is the word *return*. We are not told why Orpah and Ruth accompany Naomi, or whether they were intending to go the entire way with her. We are told the reason for Naomi's return. She had heard the news that God had once more provided for the people back home. Naomi's view of God is quite bleak as we shall see. God, for her, is one who withholds and provides; and she is not happy with this picture.

The story of Ruth is told with exquisite skill. One wordplay that is evident in the opening lines is related to names. Nearly every verse contains more than one name, and this is one of the few places that the story is so encumbered. Names in Hebrew carry meanings that we need to translate. *Bethlehem* in Hebrew means literally "house of bread" (or "house of food" since the same Hebrew word serves for both bread and food). So, the information about a famine in Bethlehem in verse 1 literally states that there was no food in a place that by its very name connotes food. In verse 6 the information Naomi receives is that there is once more *bread* in the house of bread. *Famine* and *bread* bracket the introduction to this story, indicating the theme of life under the threat of death that will dominate the tale. The name of Bethlehem is not repeated in verse 6 where the reference is instead to God's people. These inhabitants of the house of bread are not just any family, they are members of God's people. Bethlehem and God's people bracket the introduction also, indicating that the events to come pertain to more than a geographical location. The small arena in which the main action of Ruth unfolds is, after all, part of a much larger history, the one that involved God's people. This type of allusion will occur again at the end of the book when the witnesses at the city gate as well as the women around Naomi refer to "Israel" (4:11, 14).

For relief the family traveled to *Moab* to find food with people who according to the tradition refused food and water to the tribes on their journey from Egypt to the Promised Land (Deuteronomy 23:3-4). The very idea of going to Moab for refuge and provisions would be ludicrous.

Elimelech, the name of the man, sounds like the phrase "my God is king." This could be another reference to a time when there was no king in Israel, that is to say not a human king. Another undertone here may be that the word *melech*, which means "king" in Hebrew, is close to the word *Moloch*, a deity of the Ammonites who would be associated with Moab also. The cult of Moloch according to the Bible required child sacrifice and was a persistent threat at the time of the two kingdoms (2 Kings 16:3; 17:17; 3:26-27; Zephaniah 1:5). Thus, the name of Naomi's husband may hint at another aspect of Moab that made it dangerous and threatening, its religious practices.

Naomi means something like "pleasure" or "delight." This name will come into full play toward the end of the chapter. Her sons' names sound like they indicate "weakness" and "sickness," in anticipation of their deaths soon to take place in the chapter. *Orpah* is associated with the "back of the neck," and *Ruth* is in sound alike to the word for "companion." Each name sets up echoes that connect it to the events that take place in the story.

The words for *husband* and *wife* in Hebrew are not distinguished from those for *man* and *woman*, and this is how my translation leaves them. Partly, the words *husband* and *wife* may lead us into making assumptions about ancient Israelite family life that are not necessarily correct. Partly, leaving the words *man* and *woman* intact helps to emphasize how much this story is about women and the way they walk on the edge of death because of the absence of male presence in their lives. Naomi is *his woman*; Elimelech is *the man of Naomi*. Naomi, *delight*, is the one who is twice left behind, once by her *man* and again by her *sons* (verses 3 and 5); and so it must be said of her that *she was left behind,... without her two children and her man.* It is interesting that in verse 5 the narrator uses a word that translates more closely to *children* than the word *sons* used in verses 1 and 3. The word for *child* is closely related to *birth-giving* and is thus used deliberately, for it is the absence not only of male children but also of the possibility of giving birth (an issue implied also in the case of Orpah and Ruth!) that causes Naomi's bitterness (verse 13).

On the Way to Bethlehem

Ruth 1:7-18

7. She went out from the place where she was, and her two daughters-in-law with her, and they went on the road to return to the land of Judah. 8. Naomi said to her two daughters-in-law: "Go, return, each to the house of her mother. May the Holy One treat you as kindly as you have treated the dead and me. 9. May the Holy One grant you rest each woman in the house of her man." Then she kissed them and they lifted their voices and wept. 10. And they said to her: "No, with you we will return to your people." 11. Naomi said: "Return, my daughters; why would you go with me? Are there yet sons in my belly that would be your men? 12. Return, my daughters, go! For I am too old to be with a man. Yes, if I thought there was hope for me and even tonight was with a man and even gave birth to sons. . . . 13. Would you wait for them to grow up? Would you keep yourselves from being with a man? No, my daughters, for it is more bitter for me than for you that the hand of the Holy One has gone forth against me." 14. And they lifted their voices and wept again. Then Orpah kissed her mother-in-law and Ruth clung to her.

15. She said: "Look, your sister is returning to her people and her god; return after your sister." 16. And Ruth said: "Entreat me not to abandon you, to turn from following you. For where you go, I go, where you sleep, I sleep; your people, my people; your god, my god. 17. Where you die, I die, and there I will be buried. Thus may the Holy One do to me, yes more, if even death will separate me from you!" 18. When she saw that she was determined to go with her, she refrained from speaking to her further.

In the first conversation of the book, Naomi remains in the spotlight as she does her best to persuade Orpah and Ruth to return to their native country, their home. The first chapter of Ruth assigns more words to Naomi than she will have in the sequel, and from her words we may gather her state of mind. She begins by thanking her daughters-in-law for their loyalty and wishing for them a new marriage, which they would need to stay alive. Naomi is concerned for the welfare of Orpah and Ruth and at the same time would like someone else to be in charge of finding partners for these two women. She urges them, therefore, *to return to the house of [their] mother,* so they may find rest, *each woman in the house of her man* (verses 8 and 9). She is concerned and wishes them well in the name of her God. The particular wish for their well-being is important in that it constitutes a desire for them to be remarried, a sign of the importance of male presence to these bereaved women.

A reproach to God is hidden in Naomi's first wish. She says: *May the Holy One treat you as kindly as you have treated the dead and me.* This is as much as to say that God should take an example from these women and that their behavior is a standard for God rather than the other way around. Throughout her appearance in this chapter Naomi will speak boldly of a God in whom she has lost trust. The bitterness to which she will attest later is already somewhat evident. In all Naomi's well-wishing there is also more than a hint of how unfavorably her own situation compares with that of Orpah and Ruth. Unlike her daughters-in-law, there is no future for her and no "rest" to be found in the house of a man.

The next speech brings Naomi's feelings about her deprivation and her bitterness toward God out in the open. She kisses Orpah and Ruth farewell but they have other ideas and tell Naomi that they will return with her to Judah. Then Naomi states in a dramatic and therefore more effective way how she sees her future as being only filled with ridiculous possibilities. Anyone who would join her, joins in her hopeless future. It was the custom in ancient Israel for brothers of deceased men to take care of the widow he left behind. Naomi will not be able to produce these brothers, not now, not ever; even if she could, it would be useless as far as Ruth and Orpah are concerned. They would be beyond childbearing years by the time the youngsters were grown. That she is comparing her case with that of the women at her side becomes clear when she speaks of her bitterness: . . . *it is more bitter for me than for you.* . . . Here too, it becomes clear that she puts the blame for her misfortune squarely on God.

We may well be shocked at Naomi's forthrightness. But in her statements Naomi appears as fully human, a person who has suffered profound loss and who has a sense of grievance because of it. Naomi does not hide her feelings, and it may be that in her words we ourselves may find a new freedom. It does not make us bad persons to be aware of feelings of unfairness in the face of loss and pain and to express these feelings.

Naomi's speech has the desired effect on one of the daughters-in-law. Orpah weeps but then presents her kiss of farewell. Ruth clings to Naomi, and her clinging is set in contrast to Orpah's kiss. The verb *cling* is the same as that used in Genesis 2:24, where the man is said to *cling* to his woman. It can also be used of people clinging to God (Deuteronomy 11:22; 30:20). In other contexts the word may have connotations of "sticking together." Intimacy, permanence, and unbreakable closeness is implied by the verb. Naomi makes one last effort, pointing out that Ruth's true companion is Orpah, her sister by marriage. Orpah has done the sensible thing, returned to where she belongs, *her people and her god.* Do the same, she urges, *return after your sister* (verse 15).

Then Ruth opens her mouth and for the first time speaks her own words in the story with a refusal to Naomi's request. As she speaks her refusal, she utters at the same time an avowal of clinging to Naomi, adding an oath to strengthen her speech, *thus may the Holy One do to me . . .* (verse 17). Ruth echoes Naomi's usage of the word *return* (translated "turn" in verse 16 for the sake of a smoother translation). Literally, the text reads: *Entreat me not to abandon you, to turn from following you.* Hereby Ruth declares that for her to *return* home would mean to abandon Naomi. Returning, in Ruth's words, equals abandonment; and she will not abandon Naomi.

We may have become accustomed to think of Orpah as the "bad" daughter-in-law, as compared to Ruth, the "good" one. The text condemns Orpah in no way; thus, we must be careful not to read condemnations into the story. You could say that Orpah is the obedient daughter and Ruth the disobedient one. The issue at stake is not obedience or disobedience, however, but that Naomi should not be left to herself and must be assured of someone's presence.

We know Ruth's words of course; we may even know them by heart. Most often we may hear them in a wedding ceremony, and indeed this text has become so identified with weddings that it may be difficult to consider it apart from that context. Yet, the situation could hardly be more unlike a marriage ceremony where two people bind themselves willingly into a union for their mutual support and benefit. With Ruth and Naomi, two people lacking status, power, and the resources to survive are bound into a union by one partner going against the counsel of the other. Two weak people do not create strength together. Ruth joins weakness to weakness, loss of hope to loss of hope.

What motivates Ruth? The text does not describe her emotions or what she is thinking. We must figure it out from her words. As she states, she considers a return to Moab an abandonment of Naomi. She may not have learned a great deal about the God of Israel, or she may have learned a lot. The text does not say. Whatever the truth may be, Ruth's actions correspond to what is expected of God's people. The God of ancient Israel is the God of loyalty, devotion, kindness, in Hebrew *hesed* (the word Naomi uses in verse 8). In God's alliance with ancient Israel there is no advantage for God. At the time of the Exodus, God *clung* to the weakest and most oppressed group around. God's people are called to show the same behavior toward one another that God showed to them. The life of *hesed* is a characteristic of the people who claim to be God's people.

The section ends with Naomi's silence. No reason for Naomi's lack of words is provided, so we are left to deduce her state of mind. From her previous words we know that Naomi is not happy, that she has no hope for the future nor for a future for her daughters-in-law if they stay with her. It is also possible that their presence in the end seemed more a burden than a blessing. As an older woman in the family circle, Naomi had responsibilities. If the young women do not go home, then it will be she, Naomi, who will have to find a home for them, and how likely is that to happen? They will be two foreign women, childless widows, from Moab, seeking to find men in Judah. Although she wished Orpah and Ruth well, it may all have seemed too much to take on. That her silence toward Ruth is one of doubt and uneasiness rather than acceptance is also borne out in the sequel (verses 19-22). But there is after all nothing more she can do in the face of Ruth's stubborn allegiance. We can almost see Naomi shrugging her shoulders as she trudges on toward Bethlehem.

This section of the story contains only one place name, but it abounds with other indicators for location. To designate the location of the women's departure, verse 7 uses the vague phrase *the place where she was*, while their destination is signaled by the place name *the land of Judah*. A place of belonging is certainly an issue in Ruth, in the sense of a place that enables life. Bethlehem, Judah, had become a place of death in the opening of the story, so a family fled to find a life elsewhere. They succeed to a certain extent, but in other ways death finds them anyway; so that in the end three women are left without male support. *The place where she was* has now become a place of death; so Naomi sets out to return to her homeland, Judah, where there is *bread* again.

When Naomi begins speaking to Orpah and Ruth, she urges them to return *each to the house of her mother* (verse 8). The place of viable life for the women is a family, since outside of the family circle, which must include the support of a male, their life is not viable. First Naomi mentions the house of their mother; but in the next breath she mentions the item that really matters to them, *each in the house of her man* (verse 9). Orpah and Ruth try to redirect Naomi's words by speaking of a return to *your people,* but Naomi will have none of it and speaks in her reply (verses 11-13) all the more forcefully of men and the importance of their absence. Naomi mentions man or men four times and sons twice, bringing the issue back to where it belongs in her perspective: for the women to have a home, to find a place of belonging, to get rest (verse 9), they will need a man. This kind of home Orpah and Ruth are more likely to find within the circle of their own people, their own culture, their own religion.

Ruth, who has her own peculiar vision on things, does not mention the word *man* once. She makes instead a ringing declaration of solidarity with Naomi, underlining the action of *clinging* to her. She sticks to Naomi; and she will continue to do so, going even beyond death. *Your people, my people, your god, my god,* she says. Whether there is a man there or not I do not know; but what I do know is that I will be at your side, you Naomi, a woman. I invoke even the name of your Holy God to swear that I will be at your side in the grave! The *place where Naomi was* did not turn out to be a place of life; and she is going back to an old home, although she expects little of her future. Ruth turns out to expect equally little of the place where she was. For her too it is a place of the dead; and she will go to a new place, although by doing so she binds her own life to Naomi's, woman to woman, instead of doing the logical thing—going toward the place where the best opportunity for life may be, that is in *the house of her man.*

The word *return* is played out to its fullest extent in this chapter. First it is used of Naomi, who is indeed going home; and so the usage in verse 7 is not surprising. Then Naomi urges her daughters-in-law three times to *return* (verses 8, 11, and 12), and also in her mouth the word means to go home. Again in verse 15, Naomi's declaration of Orpah's return to Moab fits this sense. In verse 10, surprisingly, Orpah and Ruth state that they will return with Naomi. It can hardly be said that for them to go to Judah would constitute a return. Ruth uses the word in another way when she says, *Entreat me not to abandon you, to turn from following you*, with *turn* acquiring the connotation of abandonment. The word *return* plays in this way on the theme of belonging, the place that one may call home, where there is life.

Home at Last
Ruth 1:19-22

19. And the two of them went until they arrived in Bethlehem. And when they arrived in Bethlehem, the whole city was astir on their account, and the women said: "Is this Naomi?" 20. She said to them: "Do not call me Naomi; call me Mara, for Shaddai has caused me great bitterness. 21. Full did I go, and empty the Holy One caused me to return. Why call me Naomi, when the Holy One has afflicted me and Shaddai has caused me evil?"

22. So Naomi returned and Ruth the Moabite, her daughter-in-law with her, who returned from the domain of Moab. They arrived in Bethlehem at the beginning of the barley harvest.

The tempo of the story speeds up once more, and we have the women in view next as they arrive in Bethlehem. Naomi causes a stir among the women who wonder, in shock, amazement, or happiness (the narrator leaves it ambiguous) whether this is indeed Naomi. In reply Naomi renounces her old name that has connotations of delight and takes a new one that is related to bitterness. Then she charges God with a fourfold charge. Twice she uses an old name for God, *Shaddai*, short for *El Shaddai*. This name is usually translated "the Almighty" but would be more properly translated with "God of the breasts"; it is a name of God that connotes motherly care and nurture. Naomi invokes this name to declare her bitterness in view of the fact that the God who supposedly provides nurture has done to her the opposite. She went away a mother, full; she came back without her family, empty. Naomi puts the entire responsibility for her precarious position in the lap of God. Nothing Ruth has said or done has caused her to think differently about her own emptiness. We must conclude that the presence of Ruth, at this point at least, has not provided Naomi with comfort, since her bleak view of God is now fully revealed and Ruth does not enter into the equation.

In the closing verse of the chapter the verb *return* is used for the last time: *Naomi returned and Ruth the Moabite, her daughter-in-law with her, who returned from the domain of Moab* (verse 22). In truth it cannot be said that Ruth *returned* to Bethlehem, because Moab was her home as the text itself emphasizes by calling her the Moabite. What then does the narrator mean to say? The word *return* can also be used in the Bible to mean "people's turning to God" and is so used by the prophets. It is at least a possibility that the narrator ends the chapter with another play on the word *return*. If much in the story concerns itself with the question of home and belonging, then here could be an allusion that Ruth has come indeed to the place of her belonging even if it is not her original home. By her way of life Ruth has shown and will show that she belongs to God's people.

The chapter sounds a note of hope at the end with the mention of the *barley harvest*. Harvest is a time of abundance, and the mention of it stands in clear contrast to the *famine* that opened the chapter. Famine has turned to harvest; there may yet be hope where all seemed hopeless. Naomi is not as empty as she claims, and there may yet be life ahead for her and for Ruth.

For Reflection and Discussion

1. The story is placed in a period of the past when anything could happen politically. This might have the effect of making people feel good about their own situation if they were listening to it from the vantage point of a fairly secure administration (Solomon). If they were, on the other hand, in a chaotic situation themselves (after the Exile), or struggling to rehabilitate themselves (the Restoration), a feeling might be created of solidarity with events of the past. This story, which will end well as they know, began under impossible circumstances after all; so perhaps they too can survive the impossible odds that are stacked against them. How do you connect with the political situation posed by the storyteller? Is your community like the days of the judges, or is it more like the days of Solomon? What about a famine? Do people still leave their countries and

families because of starvation and famine? Have you yourself experienced a famine or extreme hunger?

2. Elimelech and Naomi's family lived in Moab as "strangers." Later, Ruth would be a stranger in Bethlehem. I state that strangers were a protected category in biblical times. What were the attitudes toward strangers at the time of Ezra and Nehemiah? (Ezra 9 and 10) Who are strangers in your community? What measures are taken to ensure them of protection and special care? Find other provisions in the Bible for the care of the stranger beside the ones listed in the Introduction (page 12).

3. This translation reads "man" instead of the more common "husband" and "woman" instead of "wife." How do you picture family structures in ancient Israel? Was there a marriage ceremony? Who lived together in a family? Did most people live in cities/towns or in the countryside? How many people lived in a city the size of Bethlehem, or Jerusalem? How many lived in all of ancient Israel? under King Solomon? after the Babylonian Conquest? in the time of the Restoration? Is male support still essential for women's survival today?

4. Naomi put the blame for her misfortune on God. Her perspective represents a common religious understanding that every good thing and every bad thing that happens to a person comes directly from God. What could be wrong with that understanding? Naomi did not try to convert Ruth and Orpah. She seems to approve of Orpah's return to "her god." Ruth's understanding of the God of Israel seems more profound than that of Naomi. Think of a time when someone who was not connected to your church or your faith showed you a deep understanding of God and your reaction to religious insights from those outside the church.

5. Naomi rebuffed the welcome of the women in her home town. How does your community treat those who have a difficult temperament, who do not always speak pleasantly? How would Naomi's speech be received in your midst? Would it be considered blasphemous? How do we speak about God and God's intervention in our lives? Make a list of things people say in relation to God when they experience difficulties such as illness, or death, or other disasters in their lives.

Prayer

God, our Maker, you created us for companionship. We thank you for the companions you have given us in our families and friends, our children, our partners, male and female, human and animal. Open our eyes to the treasure of lives lived in community with one another and with all earth's creatures. Loving God, we grieve for those whose lives were taken from us, who no longer walk by our side. May our sense of emptiness not overwhelm us or blind us to the love from companions still present to us and to the new presence of others. Amen.

CHAPTER 2
A WOMAN'S WORK
(RUTH 2)

EASILY DIVIDED INTO THREE UNITS, CHAPTER 2 COMPRISES IN ITS MAIN part Ruth's encounter with her new world (2:3-16). This section is framed by two units, unequal in length, with Ruth and Naomi in the center of attention (2:1-2 and 2:17-23). The entire chapter opens with a verse that provides new information on Naomi's family, information that has the potential for improvement of Ruth and Naomi's situation and thus continues the note of hope with which the first chapter ended. It is not clear whether Naomi is aware of the relationship to Boaz (2:1-2). Ruth takes the initiative in seeking to provide the necessary sustenance for her small community and goes out to glean behind the reapers, one of the few means available to her of supporting herself and her mother-in-law (2:3). As she is in the field of Boaz, the owner meets her there, speaks kindly to her, and treats her generously (2:8-16). His treatment raises the expectations of the readers since they know of the relationship in which Boaz stands to Naomi. On Ruth's return to Naomi, the two have a conversation (2:17-23) during which Naomi spells out the obligation that Boaz carries because of his relationship to her family (2:20). Naomi has come out of her despondency and unawareness of the potential in her surroundings. Keywords from the first chapter are pursued in this part of the story, and new word-trails are laid to be followed up in the rest of the story. For the first time in the story the word *redeemer* occurs, a word that will find its full deployment in Chapter 3.

Provisions for Community
Ruth 2:1-2

1. Naomi had a relative of her man's, a man of power and wealth, of the clan of Elimelech, and his name was Boaz. 2. Ruth, the Moabite, said to

Naomi: "Let me go and glean grain behind someone in whose eyes I find favor." And she said to her: "Go, my daughter."

Chapter 1 told of the establishing of a community between Ruth and Naomi, on Ruth's initiative, against the odds. Chapter 2 goes on to tell of the upholding and maintenance of this community. Ruth's activities will have to support her speech to Naomi on the road to Bethlehem (1:16-17). It is not sufficient to speak of community; community must be lived. Community is also of vital importance. Without it, Naomi and Ruth's chance of surviving would be slim. Community is not always established between natural allies. Although Naomi and Ruth exist in a family relationship that binds them together, Ruth's chances for survival would have been better with her community of origin back home in Moab. In many ways, Ruth has done an "alien" thing by allying herself to Naomi; and she engages herself in enormous risk in regard to her own welfare. Yet, her alliance with Naomi will prove to be life-giving for both of them.

The first necessary action for their small household was the provision of food. Ruth must have been informed of the custom for harvesters to leave extras for the indigent (Leviticus 19:9-10; 23:22; Deuteronomy 24:19-22). She suggests to Naomi that she will go out and gather the extras, glean, at a place where someone will allow her to do so. The phrase in verse 2, *someone in whose eyes I find favor,* will be used again by Ruth when she encounters Boaz. Naomi's reply to Ruth is brief, implying a curt or resigned tone; she gives no elaborate wishes, no warnings, no advice, just a short consent.

The opening verse of this episode announces that Naomi is not as alone, not as *empty,* as she may have thought. There is a relative, that is to say someone with responsibilities toward her from the larger family circle of her deceased husband. This relative is, moreover, wealthy and influential; some translators render the Hebrew phrase used here with *a man of substance.* On Naomi's part there seems to be, at least for the time being, a lack of awareness of the relationship and its possible advantages. She would certainly have counseled Ruth to go in the direction of Boaz's property had she been "on top of things."

The opening verse is filled with references to males and to male power. The relative, who is a powerful and wealthy *man,* is actually a relative of Naomi's *man,* who is, redundantly, identified by his name *Elimelech* (a name that points to the rule of God), and the rich man's name is Boaz (which connotes something like "in him is strength"). Directly following these references, one finds *Ruth, the Moabite*, a mention that offers an almost jarring note of discontinuity. Here is a mention of the return of hope with emphatic links to the males in Naomi's life; and it turns out that for all practical purposes there is only Ruth, a widowed woman like herself, who is a Moabite.

Ruth's national origin will be repeatedly mentioned in the book, and we must assume that the writer used this indication deliberately. I have already mentioned the negative perspective that an ancient Israelite would have on Moab. More precisely, the connotations raised by the mention of Moab are those of illicit sexuality (Genesis 19:30-38; Numbers 25:1-4) and the withholding of food during the time of the Exodus from Egypt (Deuteronomy 23:3-6). The forbidding words of Deuteronomy 23 are, "You shall not seek their well-being and their prosperity all your days for ever" (verse 6).

The purpose of the writer calling Ruth "the Moabite" long after the fact of her nationality has been digested (and has been well lodged in the reader's mind) is not entirely clear. Is the signal one of sexuality and *illicit* sexuality at that? She is, after all, a Moabite! Or is the emphasis on Ruth's faithfulness and loyalty, ***in spite of*** her being a Moabite? Is the emphatic reference to Ruth's foreignness intended to speak against prevailing attitudes of xenophobia, as in Ezra and Nehemiah's time? Is there an implied irony that the one who goes looking for food belongs to a community that was not well known for its generosity? All of these are possible, and we may need to keep them all in mind as we continue to explore the story.

Favor in the Field

Ruth 2:3-16

3. And she went and arrived, and gleaned in the field behind the harvesters, and luck landed her on the plot of land of Boaz, who was from Elimelech's clan. 4. And see, Boaz had arrived from Bethlehem, and said to the harvesters: "The Holy One be with you!" And they said to him: "May the Holy One bless you!" 5. And Boaz said to his young man, the overseer of his harvesters: "Whose is that young woman?" 6. And the young man who oversaw the harvesters answered: "That is the Moabite young woman who returned with Naomi from the domain of Moab. 7. She said: 'Let me glean and I will gather grain behind the harvesters.' She came and stood from morning until now, without resting even for a moment."

8. Boaz said to Ruth: "Listen well, my daughter: Do not go to glean in another field and do not leave this one, but cling to my young women. 9. Keep your eyes on the field they harvest, and follow behind them. Have I not commanded the young men not to touch you? When you are thirsty, go to the vessels and drink what the young men will draw." 10. She fell on her face, and bowed to the ground, and said to him: "Why have I found favor in your eyes, that you would notice me? And I a foreigner!" 11. Boaz answered her: "It was told, yes told, to me, all that you did for your mother-in-law, after the death of your man; you left your father and your mother and the land of your birth and went to a people you knew not yesterday or the day before. 12. May the Holy One recompense your work and may full reward be yours from the Holy One, the God of Israel, under whose wings you have come for refuge." 13. She said: "May I find favor in your eyes, my lord; for you have comforted me and have spoken to the heart of your handmaid, and I am not like one of your handmaids."

14. Boaz said to her at mealtime: "Come closer and eat from the bread. Dip your bite in the sour wine." She sat beside the harvesters and he heaped up for her parched grain; and she ate and was satisfied and had leftovers. 15. And she arose to glean; and Boaz commanded his young men: "Also between the sheaves let her glean and do not shame her.

16. Also, pull some out for her from the handfuls and leave it; she will glean and you will not harass her."

Though Naomi, through forgetfulness or oversight, neglected to mention the important connection to Boaz, luck guides Ruth to his very property. It may be that the mention of luck at this important juncture in the story is supposed to evoke a smile from the readers who know better than to think that luck is in charge of the events here described or in their own lives. It is also possible that the writer offers a subtle contrast to Naomi's view of things. Naomi has ascribed everything to God, both good and bad, especially bad. She has assigned her misfortune directly to the hand of the Almighty. It could be that the story at this point offers the possibility of a God who is not directly involved in the daily affairs of God's people. The task of working out the life of a faithful member of God's people is their responsibility and, of course, it helps if luck has a hand in it. Naomi may be seen by the narrator as being all too quick to assign blame or blessing to God.

The major scene of the unit portrays the meeting of Ruth and Boaz in the field with its own introduction and conclusion. Boaz arrives and, after exchanging proper greetings with his workers, inquires regarding Ruth's antecedents and receives information about her (verses 4-7). These verses form the introduction to the exchange that takes place in verses 8-13. Boaz speaks kindly to Ruth and in a slightly elevated style. He urges her to stay on his property where he can make sure her safety is guaranteed; he advises her to *cling* to his young women and to drink when the young men draw water. It is clear from his words that *young men*, male workers in the fields in this case, are not entirely safe for Ruth to be around. They will leave Ruth alone on Boaz's command *not to touch her*. Ruth will work under his protection. The word *cling* is the same as that which was used of Ruth's clinging to Naomi. The young men are not to *touch* Ruth, and she is to *cling* to the young women of Boaz. Ruth had clung to Naomi without advantage to her position. This time, her clinging to those of her own sex will enhance the promise of safety. Does Boaz also mean to limit somewhat Ruth's circle of interest to his own benefit?

Ruth, in return, is properly deferential and grateful. In her response to Boaz she wonders why she has *found favor* in his eyes, and she refers to herself as a *foreigner*. Whether her question is genuine or not, it has the result of turning our attention to the issue that much will depend on whose favor Ruth will manage to find. It also has the result of stretching the conversation between Ruth and Boaz since he will need to answer. Her self-reference as a foreigner is not wrong, but it is not accurate either. The position of outsiders in ancient Israel was carefully designated. A foreigner, as indicated with the term here used in Hebrew, would be someone from another group or nation who is around for a temporary stay only, someone who is passing through. This is definitely not the case for Ruth, who is in Judah to stay by her own avowal. In that case she should be called a stranger, in Hebrew a *gera*. Strangers are those who have come from the outside to live with the community for an indefinite time and who can count on the laws to protect them, on provisions to be made for them as they were required of the ancient Israelite community. It could be that the narrator here depicts Ruth's ignorance, but that would be a singular example in a woman who throughout the story acts with consistency and perspicacity and who seems to be well informed of her rights.

It is also possible that the word *foreigner* is used at this point to set in relief Boaz's response, which could be heard as, "I know full well what you have done; don't come claiming foreigner status to me!" Boaz's reply refers implicitly to Abram's leaving his family and land of birth on the call from God to the Land of the Promise (Genesis 12:1) and thus puts her in a line with patriarchal tradition. He then adds words of blessing, echoing Naomi's words to Orpah and Ruth on the Moab/Judah road (1:8-9) although not as specific in his wishes as Naomi. His phrase *under whose wings you have come for refuge* establishes a new word-trail that will find a resolution in another episode.

Ruth counters with a third reference to her *finding favor*; perhaps we should read here *May I continue to find favor*. She also assures Boaz that he has spoken to her *heart,* a phrase that occurs elsewhere in the Bible in connection with wooing a woman, although in every case the circumstances of the wooing are colored by past or future disaster (Genesis 34:3; Judges 19:3; Hosea 2:16). *Comfort* is linked with male-female relationships in the story of Isaac and Rebekah, when Isaac is said to have been *comforted* because of Rebekah and his love for her (Genesis 24:67) and in the Judah and Tamar story (Genesis 38:12, see footnote in NRSV). Comfort is usually given and taken in a context of loss (see also Jeremiah 31:15, 16-20). Taken together these references hint both at Ruth's status of deprivation and at the potential of Boaz as a future husband for Ruth. Her statement about her servant status is usually taken to be one of deference: I am not *even* one of your maidservants! It is also possible that it is a straightforward statement: Ruth declares that she is not in a servant-master relationship with Boaz. Does she imply that she can be more than a servant to Boaz? Time will tell.

Mealtime arrives, and Boaz adds kind and generous deeds to his words. On his invitation Ruth takes her seat at the board of the workers. Boaz passes food her way and later makes it possible for her to do more than pick up a few extras by telling his workers to leave extras on purpose (verses 14-16). Concretely these opportunities mean that Ruth not only does not have to do her work on an empty stomach but that she has enough for extra energy and some to take home. Symbolically, into a life that was deprived of sustenance, marked by absence of persons and things that provide support and make life possible, now have come "extras." In this part of the story Ruth receives not just enough to get by on but more than enough to go on with, signs perhaps of better times yet to come. *She ate and was satisfied and had leftovers* (verse 14).

The Man Is One of Our Redeemers
Ruth 2:17-23

17. And she gleaned in the field until evening, when she beat out what she had gleaned, and it was about an ephah of barley. 18. Then she took it and arrived in the city. And her mother-in-law saw what she had gleaned. She brought out and gave to her the leftovers of the meal. 19. Her mother-in-law said to her: "Where did you glean today and where did you work? May the one who noticed you be blessed!" And she told her mother-in-law where she had worked and she said the name of the man where I worked today is Boaz. 20. And Naomi said to her daughter-in-law: "Blessed be he by the Holy One who has not abandoned his kindness to the living and the dead"; and Naomi said to her: "The man is our relative, he is one of our redeemers." 21. Then Ruth, the Moabite, said: "He also said to me: Cling to the young men that belong to me until they finish with all my harvest." 22. Then Naomi said to Ruth, her daughter-in-law: "It will be well my daughter if you go out with his young women, and they will not molest you in another field." 23. And she clung to Boaz's young women to glean until the end of the barley and wheat harvests. And she stayed with her mother-in-law.

Ruth has a heavy load to haul home. Although we are today not sure of the exact measure of the ephah, it weighed somewhere between thirty and fifty pounds. It is therefore immediately obvious to Naomi how well Ruth has done, and her astonishment causes her to snap out of her despondency and bitterness. She is now as eloquent in praise as she was once in denouncement. Twice she utters the word *blessed*. She, who once accused God of wounding her, now blesses the God who has not abandoned *kindness*. The Hebrew word *hesed* is the same word Naomi used when she wished that God would treat Orpah and Ruth as *kindly* as they had treated her and her family. The concept of *hesed* was important for ancient Israel's understanding of God and itself. Sometimes English translations render it with "steadfast love." God is abounding in *steadfast love*

(Exodus 34:6; Psalm 103; Jonah 4:2). In the covenant community *hesed* was also required from one member to another. For a community to exist in health, in the Bible called *shalom* (devotion to each other's welfare), *hesed* must be practiced actively. Ruth has shown already that she lives according to the way of *hesed* in her relationship with Naomi.

In addition to her praise of God's kindness, Naomi reveals important information about Boaz by saying that he is one of *our redeemers*. This term indicates that he is more than a relative, he is a relative with legal responsibilities toward destitute family members (see page 13). We notice also that Naomi uses the pronoun *our* including Ruth in the potential benefits. The impact of this revelation is twofold: it raises new hopes for the future, and it makes one wonder about what Boaz has done so far for Ruth.

Unlike Chapter 1, Chapter 2 is full of words with positive connotations. Words for gleaning and harvest abound. *Kinsman, relative,* and *redeemer* are words that play a prelude on the positive turn of events to come, when the emptiness of Naomi and Ruth will be filled for good.

Once more, important information about the characters and their relationship toward each other is indicated by the way they are named in the text. The chapter opened with identification of Ruth as *the Moabite*, while Naomi is simply referred to by her proper name. In the closing lines of the chapter, Naomi is called *her mother-in-law* four times, and Ruth is twice identified as *her daughter-in-law*. The reader already knows of this relationship; and from the point of view of information, these identifications are unnecessary. The emphatic way in which these terms are used indicates that the relationships of the story are at this point highlighted. Naomi has, until now, not acted positively on her relationship with Ruth. In this brief section, her utterances are made as those of a mother-in-law who no longer only sees emptiness in her future but who is beginning to spot a glimmer of hope precisely in relation to Ruth, her daughter-in-law. These identifications serve to underline a turn in Naomi's outlook.

The information about Boaz as one of the redeemers is carefully withheld until the end of the episode. Ruth had gone into the field of Boaz, as luck would have it, to see if she could *find favor* with someone; and she had indeed done so. Boaz had gone out of his way in kindness and generosity toward Ruth, providing for her at mealtime, protecting her in the field, and safeguarding her gleaning. Yet, when Naomi remarks on his status as a redeemer, one cannot help but wonder. Surely, Boaz himself must have been aware of the fact. Then why has he not acted as a redeemer? The duties and responsibilities of a redeemer went much further than the generosity Boaz showed to Ruth in the field. Among all the positive notes of this episode, there is then an undercurrent of doubt. Will this Boaz come through? Also, in the last verse the words *the end of the . . . harvest* sound a foreboding note. At the end of the harvest, matters have not changed for Ruth and Naomi; and they are not any less dependent on the goodwill of others than they were when the chapter opened. Boaz has not gone beyond his generosity to act truly as *one of our redeemers.* So far Boaz does not seem to have the hang of the life of *hesed,* of providing the *extra* required of the people of God. Does he need some prodding in the right direction perhaps?

For Reflection and Discussion

1. Read Leviticus 19:9-10; 23:22 and Deuteronomy 24:19-22. What word would you use to describe the provisions prescribed in these texts? Is it enough in a community to make provisions of this kind? To what actions would you compare harvest leavings in your own context?

2. What elements constitute a community? How does a community differ from a group, on the one hand, and from an institution on the other? How is the concept and practice of community essential to your faith?

3. Bring some barley and/or wheat into the discussion group and feel the texture of each. How are these grains used today?

4. Think of names of women who are or were important to you. Write them on a piece of paper in big letters and put them in a place where everyone in the group can see and read them. Recite the names aloud. At the end of your discussion, recite a prayer incorporating the names.

5. In verse 21, Ruth cites Boaz as having told her to *cling to the young men.* That is not what Boaz said to her in verse 8. What reason could there be for this substitution? How does Naomi's reply fit with Ruth's remark? What might Naomi's tone have been?

Prayer

Holy God, our companion and keeper, forgive our zest for competition and strife; create in us a desire to walk with one another as loyal companions, as once Ruth walked together with Naomi and created a path toward a new home. Awaken in us an awareness of the needs of those who are close to us and who fill us with energy to seek provisions for community. Amen.

Chapter 3
A Woman's Power
(Ruth 3)

Like the previous chapter, this episode centers on Ruth and Boaz (verses 6-15) framed by conversation between Ruth and Naomi (verses 1-5; 16-18). In line with having turned to a more active self, Naomi has a plan to propose to Ruth. It is now the end of harvest and winnowing time. Soon, the days are going to be over that Ruth will bring home a supply of food. If Ruth will go down to the threshing floor and lie down beside Boaz, who in a tired and inebriated state would be unlikely to go home to Bethlehem, all will follow from there. Ruth prepares herself for what must have been a risky adventure, and she does as her mother-in-law has instructed her (verses 1-5). Once Boaz has discovered her, she announces her identity and makes him a proposal. Boaz wants to do as she asks, but there is another person who has rights to redemption duties before him. Words for *redeem* and *redeemer* come into full play in this section. Boaz also lavishes Ruth with praise, makes sure that she goes home before it is completely light so that no one will recognize her, and provides her with extra food to take home to Naomi. The concluding conversation between Ruth and Naomi is brief but contains important keywords.

Naomi and Ruth at Home

Ruth 3:1-5

1. Then Naomi, her mother-in-law, said to her: "My daughter, should I not seek for you a home that will be good for you? 2. Now, is not Boaz, our relative, with whose young women you were? Look, he will be winnowing barley on the threshing floor tonight. 3. Now, wash and perfume yourself, and put on your cloak; go down to the threshing floor and do not make yourself known to the man until he has finished eating and drinking. 4. Then when he lies down, get to know the place where he lies; then go in and uncover the place at his feet and lie down; he will tell you what you should do." 5. She said to her: "All that you say to me I will do."

Seven weeks have passed. The women have lived together, Ruth going out each day to provide for their short-term needs. Seven weeks, and not much has changed in respect to their long-term needs. The harvest is in, time for the threshing and winnowing; and Ruth will no longer be able to go and glean. Naomi has had ample time to think of some way to take advantage of an inauspicious moment, *the end of the . . . harvest.*

As long as there was work to do, the future seemed to hold some promise at least; as long as someone prepared to go out each day to provide for the household, life seemed possible. Women are sometimes described in the Bible as busy housekeepers, in charge of servants, provisions, and doing business (1 Samuel 25 and Proverbs 31:10-31). In such descriptions, however, women function within the accepted structures of the household with a man as its head. Ruth and Naomi function without this support; and they need to rely on their own inventiveness to move things along, once the breadwinning activity is cut off.

Naomi takes the initiative. Her outlook is so changed that she has become aware of her own responsibility in regard to Ruth; it appears that they cannot rely on their *redeemer* Boaz to go further than he has done. Her phrase *should I not seek for you a home* (verse 1) echos words she spoke earlier to her daughters-in-law on the Moab/Judah road when she wished for them *rest* in the house of a husband (1:9). The words used here for *rest* and *home* are closely related in Hebrew. In other words, Naomi is contemplating a suitable marriage for Ruth. Everything she says to Ruth should be seen in this light.

Boaz is the most suitable candidate, but he does need some prodding indeed. So far, nothing has happened beyond his initial expressions of concern. Therefore, Naomi instructs Ruth to find Boaz at the festivities surrounding the winnowing, to lie where he lies down, and to await his instructions. All Ruth will have to do is to be at the right place and listen. Boaz will take charge at that point: *He will tell you what you should do* (verse 4). Ruth replies obediently: *All that you say to me I will do* (verse 5).

There is risk in this plan. The dangers to Ruth's well-being are great, and on Ruth's welfare Naomi's welfare depends; that much is now clear. It is also clear that Ruth has a strong mind of her own and the power to make her own decisions. For her to agree with the plan means that she consents to carry it out. She has not always followed the advice of her mother-in-law, but this time she goes along. She must weigh the risk of the trip to the threshing floor against the risk of continuing their life together without male presence, and the second is greater than the first.

There are allusions to sexual activity in this section: the verb *to know* coupled with *lie down* hints at more than affable sharing of a sleeping spot; *the place at his feet* also hints at more than the obvious meaning, since *feet* can be used as a euphemism for male genitals. Mother Naomi has more in mind than she spells out, and Ruth as a careful listener certainly must have received the message. A sexual encounter might have the desired consequences. On the other hand, Ruth may be able to turn the situation to her advantage without more risk to herself than necessary. Her words to Naomi should put us on guard, for they sound suspiciously meek.

A Call on the Threshing Floor
Ruth 3:6-15

6. And she went down to the threshing floor and did according to all that her mother-in-law had commanded her. 7. And Boaz ate and drank and he felt good and went to lie down at the edge of the grainheap and she came secretly and uncovered the place at his feet and lay down. 8. Now in the middle of the night the man shivered, groped around, and, look, a woman was lying at the place at his feet! 9. He said: "Who are you?" She said: "I am Ruth your servant; spread your wing over your servant, for you are a redeemer." 10. He said: "Blessed may you be by the Holy One, my daughter! You have done a second deed of kindness better than the first by not going after the young lads whether poor or rich. 11. Now, my daughter, do not be afraid, all that you say I will do for you, since all my people know that you are a woman of power. 12. And now, while in truth I am a redeemer, there is a redeemer closer in line than I. 13. Spend the night, and if in the morning he will redeem you, fine, let him redeem; but if it does not please him to redeem you, then I will do the redeeming, as the Holy One lives! Lie down until morning."

14. She lay down at the place at his feet until morning and arose before people could recognize each other, for he thought: "Let it not be known that the woman came to the threshing floor." 15. He said: "Bring your wrap which you have on, and hold it out." So she held it out, and he measured off six measures of grain and put it on her. And she went to the city.

Harvest time everywhere is always party time. In Bethlehem of more than two and a half millennia ago things were not so different from the countryside of my youth, where the owner of the orchard was expected to join the workers in their celebration, once the fruit was picked. Boaz has drunk enough to be feeling good. Often this expression carries the connotation of a state of slight inebriation, sufficient so that judgment may be impaired (1 Samuel 25:36; 2 Samuel 13:28; Esther 1:10).

Ruth comes *secretly*, lies down at the place Naomi had indicated, and so it seems as if she is indeed doing everything Naomi told her to do. In the middle of the night, Boaz has a spasm, perhaps from a dream, and moves or gropes around; so he wakes up, finds Ruth, and asks who she is (verse 8). Ruth reveals her name, the only time her name is used in the section, which avoids the use of either her or Boaz's personal name, calling them instead *the man* and *a woman*. Ruth adds the identification *your servant*. Instead of calling herself *the Moabite* or *Naomi's daughter-in-law*, she refers to herself directly by her name and then puts herself in relationship to Boaz: *your servant*. Her next words, together with her words of self-identification, the only words she speaks during this encounter, are *spread your wing over your servant, for you are a redeemer* (verse 9).

When Boaz had met Ruth in the field at the beginning of the harvest, he had spoken kindly to her. Among other things, he had said: *May full reward be yours from the Holy One, the God of Israel, under whose wings you have come for refuge* (2:12). In the Bible the wings of God are a symbol for God's protective power (for example: "Keep me as the apple of your eye / hide me in the shadow of your wings," Psalm 17:8). Boaz draws on this image when he utters his wish to Ruth in the field. Ruth, in her turn, uses the phrase to point out that such a wish is empty unless the one who utters it is willing to cooperate with the task of protection. "You, Boaz," she says, "are the one who will actually have to step in and do the work." With the words *you are a redeemer*, she calls on Boaz as the one who has the responsibility to protect, one of the primary tasks of the redeemer in ancient Israel.

In most English translations of the Bible, the word *wing* of verse 9 is rendered with *skirt*; and the phrase then reads *spread your skirt over your servant*. Although the Hebrew word allows for such a translation, it robs Ruth of the religious insight she conveys by means of her pun. The protection of God has to be brought into operation by a human being, Boaz. Just as Ruth did not send Naomi back to Judah with God's blessing but instead ***became*** God's blessing to Naomi, so Ruth asks that Boaz do the same for her.

On a practical level, Ruth requests an intimate relationship in such an ambiguous way as to leave the choice up to Boaz. The symbol of the wing/skirt is used elsewhere in connection with illicit sexual relations (Deuteronomy 22:30; 27:20, see footnote in NRSV) or with betrothal (Ezekiel 16:8). Ruth has gone far beyond her promise to Naomi that she would do all Naomi told her and, by implication, wait for Boaz to tell her what to do. She proposes to Boaz and at the same time provides him with religious and moral reasons for going along with her request.

Boaz's response to Ruth is entirely positive. He calls her *blessed* and labels her as a *woman of power* (verse 11), using the same word applied earlier to himself when he was introduced as a *man of power* (2:1). The word *power* is seldom found in the Bible linked to a woman. Power of character is what is indicated, the power of character that exhibits itself in deeds as well as words.

In these verses the word *kindness*, Hebrew *hesed*, is heard for the last time in the book. Once Naomi wished that God's kindness would correspond to the kindness of her Moabite daughters-in-law; once Naomi blessed God for divine kindness in putting Boaz in their path; now Boaz praises Ruth's *kindness*. Ruth has once more proved she is willing to give the extra, more than what is required of the people who model their behavior on God's behavior.

Looking once more at the events as they are described here, we may well be astounded at Ruth's courage. She, as an unattached Moabite woman, goes out under cover of darkness to a place of public celebration to look for a man. When the moment is right, she lies down next to him and, on being discovered, proposes marriage or sexual relations. Even by today's tolerant standards, there would not be a great deal of approval for the woman in these circumstances. Had she been raped, public opinion would most likely be that "she asked for it." The risks for Ruth were great.

A trip alone to the threshing floor in the dark would mean a risk of being molested. Safely at the place of her destination, she might be discovered by others, who might expose her. Boaz, once he found out who was at his side, might not be friendly at all. He might send her home with disapproval, curses instead of blessings.

Boaz, however, pours extravagant praise on Ruth and assures her with the words *all that you say I will do for you* (verse 11), with an ironic twist on a phrase used twice in this chapter already. Naomi had told Ruth that Boaz would tell her what to do (verse 4), to which Ruth responded *all that you say to me I will do* (verse 5). It turned out that Ruth did not quite do all that Naomi told her, or rather that she did more than Naomi told her, acting on her own initiative in typical Ruth-like fashion. Then, instead of Boaz telling Ruth what to do, he assures her that he will do all she says. This play with a phrase is deliberate and emphasizes the autonomy with which Ruth acts, an autonomy fully approved in the story.

Once he has reassured her, Boaz reveals a new piece of information: *there is a redeemer closer in line than I* (verse 12). There was, most likely, an established order of people in a clan to whom the redeemer's duty fell. To the one closer in line the option to redeem should be offered first. Perhaps Boaz, like Naomi, had been pondering a way to get closer to the possibility of the redemption duty; and here is his chance! In addition, the introduction of the redeemer who is closer in line adds an element of suspense. Without his presence, the story would be over at the end of Chapter 3. Because of the near-redeemer's existence, we are not quite sure that events will develop entirely to satisfaction.

Like Ruth, Boaz is circumspect in his speech. His phrasing *if . . . he will redeem you, fine, let him redeem* does not clarify what the redeeming will involve. Ordinarily it would have been a question of land redemption; and marriage would not come into it, since the two customs were not linked in biblical times. Ruth has connected the two items, however, so it is possible that Boaz hints at marriage as well as property. Words for redeeming abound in this section. In verses 9-13 they occur seven times, six of these put in the mouth of Boaz. It is as if he intends to reassure Ruth that he knows what he is talking about when it comes to redemption responsibilities, perhaps because he has not given that impression until this point in the story.

Next, Boaz acts to prevent people from talking about Ruth in a way that she would be implicated in scandal. She lies down but leaves him before it is light so that what she has done will not become public knowledge. From a practical, and more selfish, point of view, Boaz may have felt that his future transactions would be in jeopardy if folks were aware of Ruth's presence with him during the night. When it is time for her to go, he gives her the benefit of his generosity.

We may be wondering whether anything "happened" on the threshing floor, just as the people of Bethlehem would have wondered had they known about it. There are certainly allusions to sexuality, some of which I have already pointed out. This section makes use of terms that continue this theme (*the place at his fee*t, *to lie down, to sleep,* and *to spend the night*). With others, I believe that the point of the narrative here lies exactly in these allusions. Sexuality and fertility are matters of great importance insofar as they will safeguard the lives of Ruth and Naomi. Eventually sexual relations will result in conception and the birth of a son. Until that moment these allusions are used in anticipation and to heighten awareness. Inference is often a more powerful literary device than graphic description.

Naomi and Ruth at Home

Ruth 3:16-18

16. She arrived at her mother-in-law's, who said: "How are you, my daughter?" She told her all that the man had done for her. 17. She said: "These six measures of grain he gave to me for he said to me: 'You shall not arrive empty at your mother-in-law's.' " 18. She said: "Stay put, my daughter, until you know how the matter falls out; for the man will not rest unless he completes the business today."

In these verses Ruth speaks for the last time in the story. Upon Naomi's question she tells of Boaz and his promise and quotes him as saying, *you shall not arrive empty at your mother-in-law's* (verse 17). Earlier the text did not record that Boaz said anything like this. That does not mean he did not say it. We do not know what he said. What we do know is that Ruth has considered the "empty" state of her mother-in-law all along. Ruth has filled Naomi's emptiness by her presence, by providing her with food; eventually her child will chase away the last shadows of Naomi's emptiness. The grain from her wrapper is a symbol in anticipation of the greater gift of her son yet to come.

We notice that in this last section the women are not called by their proper names. They are named only in relation to each another or by the feminine pronoun *she*. Not only Ruth but now also Naomi has acted as one standing in close relationship to another woman. Ruth's name sounds only once in this episode, as she identifies herself at the grain-heap to Boaz (verse 9). The use of feminine pronouns also sets in relief the word *man,* here used twice to indicate Boaz (verses 16, 18). The presence of a man is now definitely on their horizon. The last word of the chapter is *today*.

For Reflection and Discussion

1. What do you think of Naomi's plan? Is Naomi careless of Ruth's safety? What does she have in mind in terms of what is going to happen on the threshing floor? Ruth's reply to her sounds suspiciously meek. Can you think of comparative acts of desperation women might engage in today to save themselves and their families? Give specific examples.
2. The threshing floor is a place of decision, of truth and testing for the characters in the story. This is true for Boaz as well as for Ruth. Can you name such a place in your own experience?
3. Ruth names herself in this episode. Her positive naming contrasts with Naomi's negative naming of herself on her return to Bethlehem. How do you experience your own name? Do you like it? Do you feel strongly about it? Is it your first (given) name or your last (family) name that you think of when you say "your own name"?
4. Boaz calls Ruth a *woman of power* (verse 11). Many English translations make a connection with "worthiness" or "virtue." Another possible translation is "a valiant woman." What is the difference between "worth/virtue" and "power/valor"? Are qualities appreciated in women that testify to their power, their valor, or their worth? Do men and women evaluate such qualities differently? Do women exercise power differently from the way men use power? Describe the difference and to what extent Ruth's behavior illustrates it. Does your culture put a high value on courage and risk-taking on the part of women?

Prayer

Splendid God, Holy Creator, clothe us with power that we too may go forth and bring about the healing of what is broken and fill those who are empty with abundance of goodness and rich stores of provisions. Out of the strength of Ruth's alliance with Naomi new possibilities were born, new hopes were raised, new life ensued. We praise you for the valor of Ruth and all like her who become a blessing to others. May we also learn this turning to all that is weak, to walk the way of the dispossessed in loyal devotion and humble courageous patience. Amen.

Chapter 4
Men's Transactions—Women's Praise
(Ruth 4)

This chapter has three unequal parts. The largest section, verses 1-12, is taken up by the negotiations at the city gate and the witnessing of the ensuing ceremony. This scene has only male characters in it, providing a jarring contrast with the rest of the book; but in the book as a whole these verses are the counterpoint to Chapter 1:1-5. The witnesses place Ruth firmly within the tradition of ancient Israel's ancestors. In so doing they call on the names of three ancestral women, drawing on some peculiar family history. A bridge, verse 13, reports on the union of Boaz and Ruth and the birth of their son. This verse leads into the second main section of the chapter, verses 14-17, in which women are in the center, forming the counterpart to Chapter 1:19-21. Here the neighbor women are around Naomi and speak their praise for God, for the child born to Ruth and Boaz, and for Ruth. Finally, the chapter closes with a short genealogy leading up to David, the king (verses 18-22). The genealogy is often considered to be an appendix, not belonging to the story proper; but it fits well with the emphasis on ancestral history in ancient Israel.

Much in these episodes compares to and stands in contrast with the material in Chapter 1. There a family almost disappears from the scene; here a new family is constituted. There male presence is gone after a few verses; here it returns in full force. There Naomi scolds the neighbor women for calling her sweet names; here the women gather around Naomi's lap to engage in praise. There Naomi's lap is empty; here it is filled.

The patriarchal reality of life in ancient Israel is abundantly clear in this chapter, although the neighbor women provide a counterpoint to this reality.

The Cost of Redemption
Ruth 4:1-6

1. Boaz went up to the gate, sat there, and look, the redeemer passed by, the one of whom Boaz had spoken. He said: "Turn aside, sit here, so-and-so," and he turned aside and sat. 2. And he took ten men, elders of the city, and said: "Sit here," and they sat. 3. He said to the redeemer: "The portion of the field that was our brother Elimelech's Naomi offers for sale, the one who returned from the domain of Moab. 4. And I said I would inform you, saying: "Buy in the presence of those sitting and in the presence of the elders of my people. If you will redeem, redeem, and if you will not redeem, tell me and I will redeem, for there is besides you no prior redeemer and I after you." And he said: "I will redeem." 5. Boaz said: "On the day you buy the field from the hand of Naomi, also Ruth the Moabite, the wife of the dead man, you buy, to establish the name of the dead on his inheritance." 6. The redeemer said: "I cannot redeem, lest I spoil my inheritance; you do my redeeming job for I cannot redeem."

The scene at the city gate is drawn in vivid detail. We may compare the place to the equivalent of a modern courtroom. Unlike the courtroom, there is no judge present, however. The characters in the drama are supposed to be knowledgeable about the customs and laws and to be able to act on them or to revise them as they deem proper. Law was a dynamic concept in ancient Israel. There were no legal documents to be consulted. Instead, trials, disputes, and transactions were settled by elders, heads of families who were the most important inhabitants of a region or town, often at the city gate (Genesis 23:10, 18; Job 29:7; Proverbs 24:7; 31:23). Boaz acts according to the practice of his time when he invites elders to sit down with him and the other redeemer.

When all are in their proper places, probably on stone seats carved into the gate itself for the purpose, Boaz guides the proceedings. First, he announces the sale of Naomi's property, which had belonged to her husband, Elimelech; and he offers the other redeemer the chance to buy it. The redeemer is willing enough, since such an acquisition might not be unprofitable. Then, Boaz attaches information about an added responsibility, the marriage to Ruth. At that prospect, the redeemer turns the job over to Boaz, which reveals the irony of his being called *redeemer* throughout the episode.

This exchange, briefly told as it is, raises a number of questions. If Naomi had property, why has this not been mentioned earlier in the story? Did Naomi know that she had rights to a field that had been her husband's? Did Boaz know about the property earlier, or did Naomi let him know about it? If she told him, when did she do so? What does it mean *to establish the name of the dead on his inheritance* (verse 5)? Why is the redeemer unwilling to take on the task of redemption if it means marrying Ruth?

To some of these questions we have better answers than to others. The information about Naomi's property may have been deliberately withheld by the narrator, as other information was held back, to be revealed at an appropriate moment. The information is brought out at this point to provide a way for Boaz to publicly introduce his marriage to Ruth.

Redemption laws about property are described in Leviticus 25:25-34. When poverty forced a person to sell property, someone from the clan, called a *redeemer*, was to buy that property. In this way, people insured keeping property within the family. The precise order of those who had the rights of redemption is not known. In the case of Boaz, there is someone who has the right before Boaz; and Boaz offers him the first option to buy the property. Probably, such property was not allowed to lie fallow; and someone else may have reaped the benefits of the land during Naomi's absence from Bethlehem (see 2 Kings 8:1-6, for example).

Another possibility is that Boaz invents the existence of property in order to bring up the issue of marriage to Ruth, which is his real objective. In case the other redeemer took on the redemption duty, Boaz could as a last resort offer a piece of his own land as Naomi's property. He was, after all, a relative of Elimelech's; and his use of the land would not be challenged. It is certain that Boaz cleverly manipulates the transaction. First, the redeemer agrees. By introducing the marriage to Ruth separately, Boaz focuses the attention of the redeemer in that direction. When the redeemer who is first in line is looking in that direction, all he sees is his inheritance; and he refuses, out of concern for that inheritance.

Actually, the text introduces two social customs in combination: that of redemption and that of so-called levirate marriage. Naomi referred to the latter custom when she spoke to Orpah and Ruth on the road from Moab to Judah (1:11-13). The marriage of a man to his dead brother's wife was a duty in Israel, most elaborately described in Deuteronomy 25:5-10. There, the widow is said to have the right to demand this duty from her brother-in-law and to take off his sandal and spit in his face if he refuses. The first-born son of the new marriage would be considered the son of the deceased man. The expression *to establish the name of the dead on his inheritance* is, therefore, synonymous with this type of marriage. Its name, *levirate*, comes to us from the Latin word for the Hebrew "brother-in-law."

In the case of Ruth, there is no possibility of brothers performing this required marriage; but the duty may have been one that could have fallen on more distant relatives in certain periods of ancient Israel's history. The result of the custom was twofold, even if its intent was one-sided: to continue the family line and to protect the life of the widow who, without husband and sons, would be left in a completely unprotected state. Although the two customs, that of redemption and brother-in-law marriage, do not occur connected elsewhere in the Bible, their connection is natural. They both concern the protection of life and property. They both fulfill the principle of care for those who are oppressed and unfortunate.

Of course, there was a price for redemption and levirate marriage. To redeem property one had to buy it. To marry a brother's wife meant that the offspring of that union would eventually inherit the deceased's property as well as a share in any property available through the brother-in-law marriage. In the case of Naomi and Ruth, the redeemer is afraid, as he candidly points out, to *spoil* his inheritance (verse 6).

Only one other story describes a case in which levirate marriage functioned in a highly important way, and it is a story that has bearing on the Book of Ruth. In Genesis 38, two men refuse their responsibility toward Tamar of the Judah family: Onan and his father Judah. Onan is the brother who has the original duty of raising offspring by his dead brother's wife, Tamar. He disobeys his father's request, however, while appearing to obey it. His reason for not complying may have been similar to that of the redeemer in Ruth, but his refusal is secretive and dishonest.

When Onan dies, Judah promises Tamar that she will eventually become the wife of Shelah, his last son, when he comes of age. As the story unfolds, it becomes clear to Tamar that Judah has no intention of marrying her to Shelah. In the end, it is Judah himself who becomes the father of Tamar's offspring, manipulated into fatherhood by Tamar, who gives birth to twins. From this story it appears, among other things, that it was at least possible for someone other than an immediate brother to perform the levirate duty. Genesis 38 is also significant for the Ruth narrative in that the offspring resulting from Judah and Tamar's union establishes the line that led to Boaz and will lead to King David (verses 18-21).

It is also evident from Genesis 38 that a rejection of the duty of levirate marriage was condemned and considered to be destructive behavior in ancient Israel. The prescribed case in Deuteronomy attaches shame to the one who refuses to do his duty as brother-in-law. No such negative judgment is apparent in Ruth. The redeemer utters his objection openly, and that refusal clears the way for Boaz to take on the task he desired.

The events at the city gate depict one of the crucial moments of the Ruth story, and actions and words are recorded in clear and minute detail. In view of this attention to detail, it is striking that the redeemer is not given a name. When he is first introduced, he is called *the redeemer . . . of whom Boaz had spoken* (verse 1). Then Boaz addresses him with an expression I have translated with *so and so* (verse 1). The Hebrew used here occurs only in a few other places in the Bible, and it certainly points to a deliberate anonymity. *So-and-so* is not meant in a pejorative sense.

The withholding of the redeemer's name is also curious in view of the fact that in this part of the story names of present and past characters abound. Here one finds out that Ruth was married to Mahlon, for example (verse 10). But precisely here the name of one important character is missing, a character who after verse 3 is simply called *the redeemer.* One explanation could be that this character, introduced so late in the story, disappears from the stage almost as soon as he appears on it. He is only a foil for Boaz, a background character, like the witnesses or the neighbor women around Naomi, all of whom go unnamed. Second, the lack of a name may point to a lack in the person. He is not able to do the "extra" that is required of the people of God. He is called a redeemer who *cannot redeem* (note the repeated usage of that phrase in verse 6). The role of the redeemer is most like that of Orpah. Orpah serves as a foil for Ruth's faithfulness; the redeemer functions as the foil for Boaz's act of redemption.

Other people whose names deserve our attention are Ruth and Naomi. In contrast to the previous chapter, they are not named here in relation to one another. Naomi is identified as the *one who returned from the domain of Moab* (verse 3) or simply as *Naomi* (verse 5), a person in her own right. Ruth is referred to as *the Moabite, the wife of the dead man* (verse 5, see also verse 10). In contrast to its definition of Naomi, the text defines Ruth as foreign and related to a male. There is no reference to Ruth as a person in her own right or as Naomi's daughter-in-law. Indeed, Ruth as a person seems to have disappeared. She is soon no longer to be Naomi's daughter-in-law, as she will be *bought* by Boaz. The use of this particular verb is jarring but reflects the reality that Ruth in her patriarchal context is in some respects comparable to property.

The keyword of the section is *redeem*. In the conversation between the redeemer and Boaz, the word is used seven times. The word *buy* supports the notion of redemption. In order to *redeem*, it is necessary to *buy*. The phrase *to establish the name of the dead* fills out the meaning of redemption. Not only property but ongoing life is involved. This one demand makes the task too great for the redeemer who is closer in line than Boaz. The last word about redemption has not yet been said, however. The idea is still to be shown in its full depth and richness. Here, the accent falls on the cost of the custom.

Witnesses at the City Gate
Ruth 4:7-12

7. Now formerly in Israel, this was the custom at redeeming and exchange: to confirm everything someone took off his sandal and gave it to his neighbor; and this was the confirmation in Israel. 8. So, when the redeemer said to Boaz: "Buy for yourself," he took off his sandal. 9. Boaz said to the elders and all the people: "Witnesses you are today that I have bought all that was Elimelech's and all that was Chilion's and Mahlon's from the hand of Naomi. 10. Also Ruth, the Moabite, Mahlon's woman, I have bought for me as a woman to establish the name of the dead on his inheritance; so the name of the dead will not be cut off from his brothers and the gate of his place. Witnesses you are today." 11. Then all the people at the gate and the elders said: "Witnesses we are! May the Holy One make the woman who comes to your house as Rachel and Leah, who together built the house of Israel. And may you be powerful in Ephrathah and renowned in Bethlehem. 12. May your house be like the house of Perez, whom Tamar bore to Judah, from the seed that the Holy One will give to you from this young woman."

This small section consists of an action with a brief explanation and two speeches. We may want to look again at Deuteronomy 25:5-10. The woman who is refused by her brother-in-law will *pull his sandal off his foot* and *spit in his face and say: "This is what is to be done to the man who does not build up his brother's house." Throughout Israel his family shall be known as "the house of him who had his sandal pulled off"* (verses 9-10). The sandal represents access or rights to property. The pulling off symbolizes the giving up of this right. The text in Ruth explains the custom in far more neutral tones than the Deuteronomy text with its strong tone of disapproval for the man who refuses his responsibility. In Ruth, the taking off of the sandal simply confirms the transaction. The redeemer himself takes off the sandal, thereby symbolizing that he hands the redemption and marriage rights over to Boaz.

The removal of the shoe is only one action necessary for the transfer of the property to become legal. The other action is that of giving witness. With the declaration *Witnesses we are* (verse 11), the transfer of the property from Elimelech's family to Boaz becomes legally valid. This function of witnesses is essential to the proceedings. Boaz's speech opens and closes with the words *Witnesses you are today* (verses 9-10). The response from those who are present confirms this declaration.

Boaz sums up the specifics to which the people are witness in terms of the acquisition of property and the possibility of continuation of the family line. We notice that the property is here referred to as belonging to Elimelech and his sons, although the acquisition is *from the hand of Naomi* (verse 9). Male presence, signified by male names, is taking over in the story. For the second time the verb *bought* is used in connection with Ruth (verse 10). The interest mentioned by Boaz is *to establish the name of the dead on his inheritance*. Not a word is said by him about the welfare of Ruth and Naomi. Naomi has disappeared behind her dead relatives; and Ruth, the woman of power, is reduced to the level of a field to be sold and bought. She has no rights at all. She is a Moabite and the wife of a dead man.

The witnesses respond to Boaz's statement with the proper formula and add their blessing. They wish for Boaz and his wife the blessing of offspring. In doing so they mention two families of the past who were crucial links in building the ancestral family and call on the names of three women, two of whom, Rachel and Tamar, gave birth after a time of infertility. By allusion, the question of Ruth's fertility is raised. The emphasis in the blessing-speech by the witnesses is on Boaz. Boaz himself expressed interest in continuing the name of the dead, but the witnesses transfer this interest to Boaz. They mention *your house* and bestow the wish *may you be powerful . . . and renowned* (verse 11).

Ruth is by the witnesses placed firmly within the tradition of ancient Israel. She has become a part of the history and the tradition of her adoptive people. Is it coincidence that the three women mentioned testify to troubled family life (Leah and Rachel) and a part of the family history that no one would mention with pride (Tamar)? Or are there hints here that Ruth may be trouble? It is certain that her name at this point is entirely erased; she is called *the woman, who comes to your house* (verse 11) and *this young woman* (verse 12). In spite of the mention of women in the ancestral traditions, the focus of this part of the story is male. This scene is the only one in the book where women are physically absent. We remember that the opening sentences of the book introduced a man and his family at center stage. It now looks as if this center is being restored. Boaz, who represents the interests of Elimelech and his sons, does not mention the interests of Ruth and Naomi.

The witnesses recall women only as they were active in building *the house of Israel* by bearing male children. The male-centeredness of a story might not be so obvious to us elsewhere in the Bible; but in the case of Ruth the story has focused on Ruth and Naomi so that now the absence of the women, their voices, their interests is jarring. But the tale is not over yet. It could have ended here or with verse 13, but another community than that of the men at the city gate will have something to say.

A Child Is Born to Naomi!

Ruth 4:13-17

13. And Boaz took Ruth and she became his woman and he came into her; and the Holy One gave her pregnancy and she gave birth to a son. 14. And the women said to Naomi: "Blessed be the Holy One who has not withheld a redeemer from you today and may he be renowned in Israel. 15. He shall be to you a restorer of life and a provider in your old age for your daughter-in-law who loves you has borne him; and she is better to you than seven sons." 16. Then Naomi took the child and put it in her lap and became his nurse. 17. And the neighbor women gave him a name, saying "A son has been born to Naomi!" And they named him Obed; he is the father of Jesse, the father of David.

Verse 13 moves the story into a fast time flow. Before we know it, Ruth and Boaz are not only married but they have a son. One sentence and more than nine months have gone by. The scene has changed from public transactions and men's affairs to family life. God, who was accused earlier of taking away life, is now credited with granting new life. Three subjects of verbs are named: Boaz, who takes Ruth and has intercourse with her; God, who grants pregnancy; and Ruth, who becomes a wife, literally *his woman*, and bears a son. The actors, each in place, each do their part; all's well that ends well, indeed.

Abruptly, the narrator puts the woman with whose emptiness the story began back in the center with her community surrounding her. Women's presence has provided life for Naomi, whether she was in a mood to acknowledge it or not. When she returned to Bethlehem from Moab, she had been unwilling to accept her neighbors' concern; and they received sharp words from her. At this moment, these women open their mouths for praise. Their first word is *blessed*. The women are not introduced; the text simply states *and the women said to Naomi . . .* (verse 14), as if they had never been absent from her. They pronounce blessings on God who *has not withheld a redeemer from you today* (verse 14).

Who is this redeemer? It could be Boaz. Boaz had truly acted as a redeemer. It could be the child who in the next verse is called a *restorer of life and a provider in your old age* (verse 15). It could be Ruth. If a redeemer is one who provides a new possibility of life, then Ruth is the one who has done this for Naomi. It could be God. After all is said and done, and human labor is past, the women turn to God with praise.

Most likely, we should consider the word *redeemer* on multiple levels of meaning, pointing to Boaz and Ruth, as well as to the newborn child and God.

In any case, the attention of the story, which seems to have shifted to men and their concerns, is back on the women. With their pronouncement about Ruth, the women make a final declarative statement that balances out the importance of men. They say that Ruth has acted out of love toward Naomi and that she is more important to Naomi than seven sons. The number seven symbolizes the ideal. In other words, the presence of one woman, Ruth, outweighs the importance of male offspring. The mention of Ruth's love for Naomi should be taken very seriously. It is the only time that the term *love* is used between women in the Bible. Until this moment, Ruth's motivation for her loyalty and kindness, her actions of solidarity and life-provisions, were not revealed. Now we are informed that she acted out of love: *your daughter-in-law who loves you . . .* (verse 15). Ruth had not acted, in the first instance, out of self-concern, nor out of concern for her dead husband; but her actions were motivated by love for Naomi. Such love, shown by one woman to another, is praised appropriately by the mouths of women.

Love between women, support among women, was apparently not a commodity easily acclaimed among the folks who produced the Bible—witness the singularity of the usage of *love* in this context. The Hebrew word *love* always points directly to loyalty and allegiance as well as to emotions. We might consider how our culture fosters or hinders love between women and thus the creation of a community of women.

Rosemary Radford Ruether writes:

> *Patriarchy has typically split women from women, across generational lines, mother-in-law from daughter-in-law in the patriarchal family, mother from daughter, women isolated in one household from women isolated in another household, women of the ruling classes from those in the servant classes. It has taught contempt for women, which women have internalized as self-contempt and mistrust of each other. It has assumed that women do not like to be with each other, are competitive with each other, and value anything a male does more than what a female does.*
> (*Women-Church*; Harper & Row, 1985; page 58)

Does our personal experience bear out the truth of this statement? It must also be said that "Women have bonded together as sisters, as adult women of the same household, as women of villages, and they have shared more than recipes and child-raising tips" (Ruether, page 58). In other words, no matter what the stereotype of "women together" may be, the presence of women to one another can be experienced as valuable, even as life-sustaining, as exemplified by the story of Ruth.

In verse 16, the child born to Ruth and Boaz is placed in Naomi's lap. Significantly, Naomi is in charge of the action: *Naomi took the child and put it in her lap and became his nurse.* She, whose lap had been *empty*, whose name had become *bitter*, is filled with new life; she has become a *nurse,* literally a word that means she nursed the child at her breast. The literal meaning is here superceded by the symbolic. Naomi is not only a life-receiver, but she has been given back the capacity to give life. The child in her lap is not just any child; he will be the grandfather of King David, the last word of the narrative proper.

Once more the neighbor women speak. Once they were reproached for naming a neighbor who had returned to Bethlehem. Now, they are the ones to give the child his name: Obed. The all-important task of naming the newborn is entrusted to the community of women that surrounds Naomi at the point of her return to life. They say, *A son has been born to Naomi!* (verse 17).

These Are the Generations

Ruth 4:18-22

18. These are the generations of Perez: Perez, the father of Hezron; 19. Hezron, the father of Ram; Ram, the father of Amminadab; 20. Amminadab, the father of Nahshon; Nahshon, the father of Salmon; 21. Salmon, the father of Boaz; Boaz, the father of Obed. 22. And Obed was the father of Jesse, and Jesse, the father of David.

It is possible that this list of "fathers" leading to David was appended to the story at a later date; it is also possible that it always provided the ending of Ruth. One of the reasons for the telling of the story may have been the retelling of the line of David. Ancestral lists are important; they remind one of the past, of who has gone before; they root us in the past and give hope for the future. Was the story of Ruth told for the purpose of tracing David's family line back to father Judah (who is not named here but who was the father of Perez by Tamar)? Did the storyteller get side-tracked into making it a story about Ruth and Naomi rather than King David's forefathers?

It is striking that in this list not a single woman's name is mentioned. If ancestral lists provide one with a past, this is hardly so for women who are not present in this ancestral recital. We must fill in the gaps by the beginning made by the witnesses at the city gate (verses 7-12), who called out the names of the women of Israel's past. We fill in the gaps by looking to the community of women around Naomi and to Ruth and Naomi themselves who surely together *built the house of Israel.*

For Christian believers, Ruth is one of the foremothers of Jesus Christ. She is one of five women named in the genealogy of Jesus in the first chapter of Matthew. The word *redeemer* in this book thus takes on another level of meaning. A story that began in desolation and bitterness finally opens up new vistas of things to come. The life restored to Naomi will result in new life indeed. Ruth by her faithfulness and love has become one of those who participate in the advent of the realm of God.

For Reflection and Discussion

1. Redemption customs and brother-in-law marriage were laws that could protect unprotected women in ancient Israel. What laws today have the same purpose? Make a list of these as they pertain to divorce, social assistance, pensions, and so forth. Do women need less protection today? How do women safeguard themselves against poverty?

2. The redeemer who is closer in line than Boaz is unwilling to pay the cost of redemption. Are there times when you feel that the "extra" required of you is just too much? Do you think God requires too much? Why or why not?

3. Summarize the ways in which the witnesses at the city gate limit Ruth as a person. In what ways do they enrich her identity?

4. The author states "love between women, support among women, was apparently not a commodity easily acclaimed among the folks who produced the Bible." What could stand in the way of women showing love for each other, then and now?

Prayer

Mother Wisdom, turn us to the way of truth, justice, and righteousness. Make us calm and patient in our endeavors so we may complete what we have begun in confidence and trust. You, who delight in the world of human children, give us a share in your joy. Jesus, our Teacher and Redeemer, walk by our side, hold our hand, dry our tears, fill our emptiness, mend our spirits, guide our feet; we turn to you as flowers turn to the sun for their very lives. We praise you and give you thanks for making manifest to us the presence of God. May our lives be filled with this gratitude, this praise, now and forever. Amen.

PART 2
THE BOOK OF ESTHER

INTRODUCTION

Date and Context

THERE IS LESS DIVERGENCE OF OPINION ABOUT THE DATE OF ESTHER than there is about Ruth. Esther certainly dates after the Babylonian Exile, in the first quarter of the sixth century B.C. By the book's own telling, the events took place during King Xerxes' reign, here called Ahasuerus—and that would put the time around 475 B.C. Most likely, the actual time of the composition was later, perhaps during the first half of the second century B.C. The background of the book then is the persecution of the Jews under Antiochus Epiphanes, who tortured and put to death Jews who resisted assimilation to Hellenistic culture and religious practices. Such circumstances of life-threatening violence make the tenor of the book understandable.

Historical evidence for the events described in Esther is lacking—and some of them would seem unlikely to the extreme, such as King Xerxes (Ahasuerus) sitting by and even rejoicing at the slaughter of his own subjects (9:12). The fact that one cannot label this book as history does not make the story untrue. Persecution of the Jews in the time of Antiochus Epiphanes and during subsequent history is all too true. The particular history of persecution and destruction of the Jewish people is the context of the Book of Esther.

Another historical tie exists in the festival of Purim, the feast of Jewish survival. Purim, celebrated in late winter or early spring, is a festival of high jinks and dress-up, when people act out the different roles of the Esther story and children walk around in costume. This context, too, is important: the atmosphere of jokes played on "the boss," or of the ones in charge "taken for a ride." It may be that at a time of great hardship a folktale such as Esther provides a community with the necessities for survival, humor, and hope.

As a small child growing up in the Netherlands during the Second World War, I heard my mother sing songs that mocked the Nazi oppressors. After the war I discovered that this type of mockery was not simply the invention of one individual. A whole body of literature had come into existence during the war (songs, stories, jokes), all ridiculing and caricaturing the German oppressors. This material was the fruit of the most serious threat to the life of individuals and communities. At the same time these stories and songs were in themselves a means for survival.

As we are accustomed in a Christian context to find Ruth in the historical section of the Bible, so we place Esther following Nehemiah. In the Hebrew edition of the Bible, Esther is placed differently. There we find the book between Lamentations and Daniel, in the latter third of the Bible called "The Writings." It may be that its placement in the historical section of the Bible has contributed to a simple historical reading of Esther that may not be the best way to understand the story. It is helpful, therefore, to keep in mind its placement in the Hebrew Bible.

Controversy and Theme

Esther is the one book in the Bible that does not mention the word *God*; further, religious practices and institutions are not mentioned even when it would be natural for the text to do so (4:15-16). The book has caused problems for both Jews and Christians alike, arising from questions of its appropriateness in the Bible. In the church, Esther is far from a favorite book for preaching or teaching. Famous theologians have expressed their distaste for this book. Martin Luther remarked that he wished Esther (as well as Second Maccabees) "did not exist at all; for they judaize too greatly and have much pagan impropriety." The festival, Purim, which seems to be the point of the story, is not one of the festivals the church adopted and adapted, as it did with other feasts of ancient Israel. Esther is a book peculiar to Jewish history, and celebrates the survival of the Jewish people by means of a woman's intercession. On top of everything, the woman, Esther, shows a great deal of bloodthirstiness when it comes to outwitting the enemy (9:12-15).

Perhaps we can turn into an advantage what seems to be a hindrance. More than any other book of the Bible, Esther faces us with the particularity of God's election, with the fact that the survival of the Jews is a theological concern. Esther provides the church with an opportunity to reflect on its relationship to Judaism and the Jews.

In Esther we learn about the features of oppression of the Jews as it took place in the Diaspora, in Persia and elsewhere, long ago and not so long ago. Esther, then, teaches also about Christian oppression of the Jewish community. As Christians, we look at a painful past in terms of our relationship to Judaism and the Jews. The church encouraged hatred of the Jews early in its history and actively participated in persecution of the Jews in the Middle Ages and Renaissance. At times, the church instigated the persecution; and it eventually contributed both actively and passively to the threat of the annihilation of the Jews in the Holocaust. The phrase to *annihilate all the Jews, from boy to old man, children and women* (3:13) creates dreadful echoes. The "once upon a time" of Esther became the time of Adolf Hitler, and the folktale turned into a horror story.

In addition, the landscape of all systemic oppression and prejudice everywhere comes into view as the Book of Esther shows where race prejudice leads. Reading Esther means looking into a mirror where we see our own anti-Jewishness and our racism. Esther herself, who was cut off from her people, provides an example of liberation through solidarity with the victims of oppression.

The Book of Esther is also about sexism, that is the ideology of patriarchy. Elsewhere I have written about Esther: "She is a member of a vulnerable class in three ways: as an orphan, a widow, and an alien who is a Jew. She functions as a female rescuer in the shadow of the banished queen Vashti. She is an alien who has to hide her particular Jewish identity. She is confined to the harem, which keeps her outside the information loop. From Esther we learn also about the possibilities of overcoming the constraints designed by a patriarchal world and may discern the design of a pattern to overcome such constraints" (*Ezra, Nehemiah, and Esther*, Westminster; page 105).

Form and Style

The main story of Esther is told in five chapters (3–7), framed by two chapters providing an elaborate introduction (1–2) and two chapters that form the conclusion (8–9). Chapter 10 forms a short postscript. The framework is constructed in an elaborate style, relying for its effectiveness on a series of vignettes described in great detail and with a tendency to exaggeration.

In Chapter 1 the length of the feast, the splendor of the palace, as well as the details of the royal administration are described in lavish detail. The same details occur in the last two chapters, except this time as they have bearing on the Jewish people. In Chapters 1 and 2 the focus is on the royal palace where the destruction of the Jews will be planned. Death hides in the shadow of splendor and beauty. In Chapters 8 and 9 the attention is on these very same Jewish people who have survived against the odds.

In contrast to the framework, the story proper is told in a more succinct style with fewer of the elaborations found in the framework. Yet, the style remains one that relies more on exaggeration and overstatement than on subtle delineation of event and characters. In this respect, Esther forms a clear contrast to Ruth.

The characters in Esther are static rather than dynamic. Once the people are introduced, they behave consistently with the way they first appeared. The king appears at first as generous, indulgent, vain, quick-tempered, gullible, and prone to too much drinking. He remains in character throughout the tale. Haman is introduced as an opportunist who has a self-image bigger than the Empire State Building, and he remains in character as well. Mordecai is solicitous, has an ear to the ground, and is clever. The exception to the more or less static character presentation is Esther herself. Esther gains in stature as the story develops. Her skill and courage and independence increase, so that she comes out in starker relief than the others. In Ruth the characters are painted more subtly, and at the same time with more depth. The characters in Esther are more like caricatures, with the exception of Esther.

Besides the four principals, there is a cast of secondary characters who set up the major roles in the story and who anticipate escalating conflict. Memucan as advisor to the king in the first chapter foreshadows Haman as a key administrator who manipulates the king into reprisals that are out of proportion to the offense committed. Vashti in the first chapter anticipates both Mordecai in her refusal to accede to the king's command as well as Esther in her growing independence and reliance on her own judgment. Vashti's fate also provides the somber background of the dire consequences that may follow an independent stand. Esther plays her role of mediator against this background.

For Reflection and Discussion

Because of space limitations, key chapters of Esther will be presented in full translation and analysis; other chapters will be reviewed and key verses translated. You will need to consult a standard translation, such as the New Revised Standard Version, for these sections of Esther.

In preparation for the study of Esther, it may be helpful to read a history of the Jewish people, as for example Chaim Potok's *Wanderings* (Alfred A. Knopf, Inc., 1978), and information on the historical relationship of Judaism to Christianity. Locate the Persian Empire on a map of the Ancient Near East, which you may find in some commentaries. Carey Moore's commentary *Esther* contains a good, simple map. You may want to do more research on the layout of palaces in that part of the world in the fourth and third centuries. J.B. Pritchard's (ed.) *The Ancient Near East in Pictures Relating to the Old Testament* (Princeton University Press, 1954) should give some ideas.

Read the Book of Esther all the way through at least once.

Questions

1. Esther is described as a "folktale." Are there other folktales in the Bible? Are there folktales outside of the Bible that remind you of Esther?

2. Recall an incident in which Jews or Judaism were denigrated in your presence. Think of subtle ways such denigration can take place. The book Christians call the Old Testament is the Bible for Judaism. The term *Old Testament* may not always be a helpful one in Jewish-Christian conversations. Can you think of some ways in which this term might be unhelpful for a Christian understanding of Scripture as well?

3. The Book of Esther was not easily accepted into the canon. (A *canon* is an authoritative list of books accepted as Holy Scripture.) Can you think of other biblical books that may have met some difficulty?

4. Discuss the implications of the following statements: (a) "The Jewish people are not rejected by God, and God's covenant is not nullified. . ." (*Reformed Theology and the Jewish People*, by Alan P. F. Sell, ed.; World

Alliance of Reformed Churches, 1986; page 34); (b) "Eligibility for the kingdom of God does not lie in sameness." Explore the implications of how you experience "difference" as a community and as individuals.

Prayer

O God, you create us in a diversity of shapes and colors. Help us to celebrate our different appearances. You create us with different talents and gifts. Aid us in making a community where each one's gifts flourish, where none are asked to produce what they have not in them to give. Help us to celebrate our different selves.

When difference frightens us, take away our fear, O friend of the fearful. When difference overwhelms us, quiet our agitation and open our eyes to beauty, O Spirit of truth.

Grant us love, and courage, and love, and patience, and love to embrace that which is not like us, O God, who became one of us in Jesus the Christ. Amen.

Chapter 1
The Court of Ahasuerus
(Esther 1-3)

Each chapter in this section contains its own tale, together providing the setting and the context for what is to follow. First, there is the lavish party of King Ahasuerus with its aftermath of conflict (Chapter 1). Parties abound in the book, and the first party is the most showy and elaborate. Festivities mixed with conflict are also typical for the rest of Esther, and this topic is efficiently introduced in Chapter 1. This first chapter also delineates the features of "the threatening other" that will dominate the sequel. Queen Vashti, her action, and the reaction to it from the palace are of more than passing importance for the tale of Esther. The second chapter tells of the attempt to replace the vanished queen and introduces Mordecai and his cousin Esther who is also his ward (2:1-7). Esther wins first place with the king through her beauty and charm so that she is made queen (2:8-18). As a tail end to the chapter, there is the discovery of a plot against the king by two eunuchs, a discovery made by Mordecai and brought to the attention of the king via Esther (2:21-23). Thus, the king's second party ends in the hanging of the villains who plotted against the king (2:23). In the third chapter, Haman enters as the fourth main character of the narrative. Haman gains the most powerful position at the court next to the king and is immediately crossed by Mordecai (3:1-3). Upon Mordecai's refusal to prostrate himself in front of Haman, Haman plots the annihilation of all Mordecai's people, the Jews (3:6-11). The decree of the impending doom of the Jews is announced in all the provinces, and the city of Susa is in turmoil (3:12-15).

A Queen Disappears
Esther 1

1. Once, in the days of Ahasuerus—he is the Ahasuerus who ruled from India to Ethiopia over 127 provinces—2. in those days when King Ahasuerus sat on his royal throne in Susa city, 3. in the third year of his reign, he gave a party for all his lords and ministers, the army of Persia and Media, and the nobles and lords of the provinces at his side, 4. while he showed off the riches and the glory of his kingdom and the splendor of his greatness for many days, 180 days actually.

5. Then when these days were over, the king gave another party for all the people present in Susa city, high and low alike, a party of seven days in the garden court of the royal palace. 6. There were white cotton curtains and blue hangings with cords of fine linen and purple wool tied to silver rings and marble pillars. There were couches of gold and silver on a mosaic pavement of porphyry, marble, mother-of-pearl, and colored stones. 7. Drinks came in gold goblets, goblets of varied design. And the royal wine was lavish as befits a king. 8. The rule for the drinking was "no restrictions!" for so the king had given orders to every steward of his household to comply with each man's desire. 9. Also Queen Vashti gave a party for the women in the royal household belonging to King Ahasuerus.

10. On the seventh day, when the king was feeling good with the wine, he said to Mehuman, Biztha, Harbona, Bigtha, Abagtha, Zethar, and Carkas, the seven eunuchs in attendance on King Ahasuerus, 11. to bring Queen Vashti before the king with her royal crown, to show the people and the officials her beauty for she was very good-looking. 12. And Queen Vashti refused to come on the word of the king that the eunuchs brought. So the king became enraged and hot with anger.

13. Then the king said to his counselors who knew the procedures (for this was the royal practice toward those who were up on law and custom—14. and his closest advisers were Carshena, Shethar, Admatha, Tarshish, Meres, Marsena, and Memucan, the seven ministers of Persia and Media who had access to the king and sat first place in the kingdom)—15. He said: "According to the law what should be done to Queen Vashti because she did not do what king Ahasuerus said by hand of the eunuchs?" 16. Then Memucan said before the king and the ministers: "Not only toward the king has Queen Vashti acted subversively but also to the ministers, and to all the people who are in all the provinces of King

Ahasuerus. 17. For word of the queen will make all women look with contempt on their husbands as they consider that King Ahasuerus said to bring Queen Vashti into his presence and she did not come. 18. On this very day the high-placed women of Persia and Media who hear of the queen's word will talk back to all the king's lords, and there will be no end of contempt and rage! 19. If it seems good to the king, let a royal word go out from him, written into the laws of Persia and Media not to be altered, that Vashti shall not come before the king again, and let the king give her royal status to another better than she. 20. And the edict made by the king will be heard in all his kingdom, vast as it is; and all the women will treat their husbands with honor, high and low alike."

21. This advice was good to the king and the ministers, and the king acted on Memucan's advice. 22. He sent dispatches to all the royal provinces, to every province in its own script and to every people in its own language: that every man should lord it in his house.

The chapter is easily divided into three parts: the first 9 verses recount the party, or rather parties, given by King Ahasuerus; then follows a section, verses 10-12, that describes the failed attempt to bring Queen Vashti into the main festivities; a final episode, verses 13-22, describes the aftermath of Queen Vashti's refusal and its effects on royal politics. The themes contained in the chapter are illustrative of what is to follow. First, we see a king involved in incredibly lavish party-giving stretching over more than half a year. The detail, the length of the party, the costly and showy decorations of the palace, all serve to give an impression of lack of moderation, unwarranted exaggeration, shortage of common sense. If the real King Xerxes had absented himself for this long from the business of ruling his extensive empire and fighting his extensive wars, not much would have been left of the 127 provinces of his realm. There is immoderate drinking going on amidst all the gaudy display: "No restrictions" was the motto! The Hebrew word for *party* is a noun related to drinking. It is no surprise that the king is *feeling good with the wine* (verse 10) at the end of it all.

Almost as an afterthought the narrator provides the information that the queen too is giving a party (verse 9) for the women of the palace. We are to conclude then that the king's party is a men's affair. As the sentence is constructed in verse 9, it is somewhat ambiguous as to what belonged to

King Ahasuerus. On the surface the reference is to the palace, but it could also be to the women. We will stay with the ambiguity, for one of the issues in the chapter is that the power of this king is defined by what and whom he controls. The beauty of the palace, the custom of the drinking, the guest list—it is all his to command. It is all his to show (verse 4).

It is natural then that the king wants to have Vashti present, and so he orders seven eunuchs to bring her so that he can *show* her as well (verse 11), for, the text continues, *she was very good-looking*. The king is *feeling good with the wine*; his queen is *good-looking*. How good can it all get? The sentence about bringing Vashti to the party stretches over two verses (10 and 11) with the words *to bring* not occurring until after the seven eunuchs have been named. There are seven eunuchs between the king and the queen's hoped-for arrival. The number of the eunuchs too seems a bit overdone. Surely, one eunuch would have been sufficient to fetch her?

Eunuchs were important personages at royal courts in the biblical world. They were involved in politics and palace intrigue besides being in charge of the harem. We will meet a number of them as the story of Esther unfolds. In any case, no matter how important they are and in spite of the fact that there are seven of them, Vashti refuses to budge. In view of the preceding elaborate phrase, verse 12 is almost laconic: *And Queen Vashti refused to come. . . .* Her motivation is not provided, and so her refusal has caused endless speculation. She may have been too busy with her own party, too tired, or *feeling good with the wine* herself; she may have thought the whole thing inappropriate, to appear as the one woman at a stag party. The text does not say, because it moves immediately to the reaction her refusal provokes in the king.

As good as he had been feeling before, Ahasuerus now feels red hot with anger; he is in a burning rage we would say. The king is mercurial, prone to quick temper changes, especially when those around him do not follow his directions. Too much wine does not help the situation, of course. So he asks his advisors (again there are seven) what should be done to Queen Vashti *according to the law* (verse 15). The queen *did not do* something and therefore something must be *done* to her. It is an interesting question; for as it turns out, there is no law against what Vashti did. Perhaps there is no law for no one had ever considered that such a thing was possible, to go against what the king *said* (verse 15).

So, the rest of the episode is devoted to the making of just such a law, a special ruling in regard to Vashti. The basis for the law is that what Vashti has done, or rather what she has not done, is far-reaching. Memucan calls it a "subversive" act, an act that not only affected the king but also was directed to every man, from minister to common folk, from ordinary husband to high-born lord (verses 16-18). When the women hear *word of the queen* (verse 17), they will *look with contempt on their husbands* and *talk back* to them (verses 17-18). To undercut that process a ruling should be made in respect to Vashti, that she *shall not come before the king again* (verse 19); and moreover the king should give her place to another. Does that sound *good to the king*? It sounds good indeed, and so the administrative process is put in gear to get the proclamations out of which the upshot is that *every man should lord it in his house* (verse 22).

So there it is. It should teach Vashti and all those like her a lesson! It all seems almost ludicrously disproportionate. All this huffing and puffing because one woman was not of a mind to come at the king's command. To forbid Vashti to come where she did not want to be in the first place, the king's presence, and to produce the grand declaration that men are lords in their household is laughable; but on the other hand, there is a deadly seriousness to the proceedings. Timothy Beal in his commentary on Esther observes that Esther is a story concerned with otherness, the otherness of Jews and women. In sexism and anti-Judaism, women and Jews are respectively projected as other. The *othering* dynamics toward these groups are interrelated in Esther (*Esther in Berit Olam—Studies in Hebrew Narrative and Poetry*, by Timothy Beal, Liturgical Press, 1999; page 1).

What we can observe in Esther 1 is the foreshadowing of much that is to come: the power of the man in charge, here Ahasuerus, later Haman, is held in place as long as there are those who are seen as and treated as "other" to control. When the control over the "other" slips over the woman (Chapter 1) or over the Jew (Chapter 3), his sense of himself slips, and strong measures must be taken to correct his sense of self. Not only is the presence of the "other" necessary for the patriarch who lords it in his house, it is also necessary to shame and humiliate the one or ones who have been relegated to "other." In this way his "honor" is upheld. The goal of the edict is that the men will receive honor from their wives (verse 20).

Thus, Queen Vashti's seemingly innocuous refusal has vast consequences and is far more disruptive than one might guess. For she is indeed saying that she is not dependent for her sense of self on the king, and that she has her own business to conduct and is a person in her own right. This resistance is intolerable in Vashti as it will be in others in the sequel. All women will suffer the consequences of Vashti's refusal, as later all Jews will suffer the same for Mordecai's refusal.

The ideology and practices ascribed to the king and Haman in Esther are ideologies and practices of male dictators and tyrants, but they are also indicative to some degree of male power in all patriarchal structures. An essential feature of the perspective is that it is unstable and that there is a chance to subvert the paradigm. Of this subversion, Vashti is the harbinger; and so Memucan was right after all. She did act subversively. Vashti's act is in the end not successful; but she has set a precedent, and others might succeed where she failed.

A Queen Appears
Esther 2

An initial section, verses 1-4, introduces a plan to replace Queen Vashti. Here is a man without the necessary "other" to make him feel good about himself. First, it sounds as if the king is beginning to feel sorry for Vashti; but before things can go too far, the servants intercede and advise the king on the right way to proceed with the replacement. The king should have a choice of *beautiful virgins* (verses 2-3); and since royal advisors are plentiful, they can be put to work to look for as many candidates as possible. If the king has a whole harem full of them, he will be able to choose at leisure and not be rushed into anything. This plan could not go wrong, no matter how you looked at it. If the first collection brought no one suitable, the advisors could get some more!

Before the wheels of the administrative apparatus are set in motion, Mordecai and Esther appear on the scene as Jews living in Susa, having ended up there because of the Babylonian Exile. They are from a generation of deportees, aliens, Jews living in the Diaspora. Mordecai is listed with a full ancestry, Esther by one name, Hadassah, which is replaced instantly with another. *He was the guardian of Hadassah, that is Esther, the daughter of his uncle, for she had no father or mother; and the young woman was beautiful of appearance and good-looking; and on the death of her father and mother, Mordecai took her for himself as a daughter* (verse 7). Mordecai's ancestry goes back to the biblical lineage of King Saul, a fact that will be of some importance in the rest of the story. Esther's beauty is emphatically stated again, the second time with the same quality ascribed to Vashti in the first chapter. Here, clearly, is a candidate for Vashti's replacement. Yet, Esther is also vulnerable; she is an outsider, a Jew, and an orphan dependent on the kindness of her cousin.

We observe that Esther is introduced by two names, the first of which appears nowhere else in the story. Hadassah may be related to a Hebrew word meaning "myrtle" and Esther to a Persian word meaning "star." Does this mean that Esther hid her Jewish name and adopted a more Persian-sounding one? Perhaps her double name highlights an ambiguous identity, at least for the time being. In the next verse Esther is taken to the palace to be prepared for eventual royal inspection: *and Esther was taken to the palace, into the custody of Hegai, the keeper of the women* (verse 8). Esther is taken from one place to another and from one guardian to another; she is not in charge of her life. She is an orphan and an alien; and the only thing she has going for her is her beauty, which as we have seen can be a liability in this kingdom.

Once inside the harem, Esther's beauty gains her acceptance from the most important person around, the eunuch Hegai; he gives her preferential treatment during the period of her beautification, which stretched over a long time. Finally, the time comes for her to go to the king's chambers; and, as foreseen, the king too falls for Esther's charms. He then makes her queen instead of Vashti, at which point it is time for another party (verse 18). The text is detailed about the length and type of beauty treatment and the specifics of the visit to King Ahasuerus. The description is so smooth that it is easy to glide over the helplessness, the boredom, and the powerlessness of the young women, each of whom waited for her *turn* (verse 15).

There are some hints that Esther is not entirely without resources. Three times she is said to *find favor* (verses 9, 15, 17). She is also still in touch with Mordecai via third parties, since the harem was inaccessible to direct contact (verse 11). On his coaching, Esther hides her identity from those around her: *Esther did not tell of her people and her birth, for Mordecai had commanded her not to tell* (verse 10). So, there she is, Esther in the harem, charming everyone in sight, without being able to tell who she truly is.

The episode of the king's search ends with the king giving another party, this time in honor of Queen Esther. As did the first party, this one ends in a punishment, albeit one that is not connected directly to the festivities themselves. Mordecai has uncovered a plot against the king by two eunuchs to assassinate the king and, through Esther, provides this information so that the culprits are punished (2:23). We note with interest that immediately before this last episode the narrator states again that Esther hid her identity for she *did just as when she was brought up by Mordacai* (verse 20). Now here is a woman who does what the men in charge tell her to do! It is now the seventh year of the king's reign (verse 16). Four years have passed since the Vashti disaster, and it does not look as if Esther will shake up the patriarchal status quo.

Enter the Villain
Esther 3

Mordecai has saved the king's life, but it is another who rises to prominence at the royal court: *Haman son of Hammedatha the Agagite*. Perhaps Ahasuerus needs a trusted man beside him in view of the treachery of the eunuchs who planned his assassination, and Haman fits the bill. His introduction as an *Agagite* connects him to King Agag of Amalek (1 Samuel 15:1-9), and this lineage puts him into opposition with anyone of Saul's lineage even before Mordecai's act of insubordination. Because Mordecai has been introduced with his full ancestry, the reader is now on guard that something is going to happen.

The honors awarded to Haman are extreme and indicate the element of exaggeration that characterizes the story. *All the servants of the king that were in the royal gate bowed down and made prostration to Haman for thus the king had commanded for him. And Mordecai did not bow and did not make prostration* (verse 2). Here is another act of disobedience. Just as Vashti's motivations for her refusal to attend the king's party were not revealed in Chapter 1, we are left equally in the dark about Mordecai's motives. It is possible that the reasons for Mordecai's refusal lie embedded in ancestry hostility. Shall this Benjaminite, descendant of Saul, bow to this descendant of Agag? Never! It could be that Mordecai had religious scruples, or that he was simply stubborn and independent, or that he had a bad back. We do not know.

What soon becomes known is how dangerous an act of insubordination this is. The servants step in and ask Mordecai why he does not obey the king's command and keep at him day after day. When he will not listen to them, they tattle to Haman. The servants may be out only to make mischief and no more than that. They know that Mordecai is a Jew. Perhaps they also know that Haman, in keeping with his ancestry, has no love for Jews. In any case, the servants make sure that Haman has all the facts. When Haman notices that there is someone who does not do him the required honor, he is beside himself, *he was filled with fury* (verse 5); and he decides that rather than punishing Mordecai alone, he will do away with all the Jews. The outrageous extent of his desire for vengeance makes it reasonable to assume that Haman fostered hatred toward the Jews even before the incident.

Once again, as in Chapter 1, a punishment is planned that seems disproportionate to the crime committed. But the disobedience is more flagrant, and the stakes are higher. Mordecai, as a member of a despised minority, one who is "other," at the expense of whose humiliation the authority of the man in charge is upheld and his sense of self is maintained, this Mordecai refuses to cooperate. Well then, he must be taught a lesson and all those of his kin with him! There is something laughable about Haman, as there is something comical about the king; but these comical figures have all the political power not only in the story but in the reality of the world of the Jews of more than 2,000 years ago.

Haman has to fix his plans and manipulate the king into giving him permission to do what he wants. Verse 7 describes his method of settling on the day of destruction. Once this practical matter is taken care of, Haman is on his way to the king. The casting of lots (in Hebrew *pur*, plural *purim*) as a technique of forecasting is lost to us; but it is clear that a propitious day is chosen by this method. It looks as if Haman takes his time until finally the *purim* fall the right way, in the twelfth month called *Adar.*

The next verses (8-11) record Haman's speech to the king; and so we pay special attention since this is the first time his words are told directly. Speech is intended to reveal to an extent a person's character, sometimes their motivations, their state of mind.

Haman's words show him to be a clever manipulator. His opening words are innocuous enough; but as his sentence goes on, the adding of a half-truth to a lie paints a picture that for a king would be threatening. *There is one people, scattered and dispersed among the peoples in all the provinces of your kingdom, whose laws are different from all people, and the laws of the king they do not obey; and it is not fitting that the king should leave them alone* (verse 8). The first four words are true enough, and the fact that this one people is scattered and dispersed is not unusual. There must have been quite a few such groups in the large Persian Empire. Yet, the information about *scattered and dispersed* adds at least one element of discomfort: These people are all over the place! The next statement is a half-truth since differences in diet and dress would constitute *customs* rather than *laws*. But Haman has to introduce the notion of *the law*, and this is a way to achieve it. Then he finishes the whole thing up with the lie that they do not obey the law of their king. It is true that Mordecai has not obeyed the edict of the king in regard to Haman, but nothing is known of a general disregard on the part of the Jews for the laws of Persia. In fact, this can hardly have been the case for a minority group that needed to survive. Timothy Beal observes that Haman has constructed "the Jewish problem" and its "final solution" at the same time.

Never mind the truth, however; Haman's speech has the desired effect on the gullible king. Of course, it is not fitting that he should let these people be! We observe that he does not even ask for a name or identity that might fit these people. It is enough to know that there are such villains around. Haman has a ready-made solution for the problem and offers the king money to make sure of his cooperation. The sum he offers is exorbitant, more signs of exaggeration; and the king consents. *The money is given to you, as well as the people, to do with as you please,* (verse 11), says Ahasuerus. One commentator translates "*Well, it's your money, said the king to Haman, do what you like with the people*" (*Esther*, ed. by Carey Moore; Anchor Bible, 1971).

The parallels with Chapter 1 are not hard to find. In Chapter 3, a person who belongs to a category of "other" disobeys the wishes of one more powerful than he, thereby unsettling the sense of control and power of the dominant one. This causes a disproportionate anger and punishment because the situation has to be rectified. In Chapter 3, as in Chapter 1, the royal apparatus is set in motion to announce the punishment; and the pogrom is announced in detail: *Letters were sent by hand of couriers to all the provinces of the king, to destroy, slaughter, and annihilate all the Jews, from boy to old man, children and women, on one day . . . and to plunder their goods* (verse 13). Such an announcement ahead of the actual event may have been intended to put the Jews in fear of their lives for a long time, something that would accord with Haman's wishes. In the story the advance notice functions as a device that makes it possible for people to prepare counterplans.

The sin of these people as Haman describes them is that they have set themselves apart. They are different—their customs are different, they look different, they eat different things, they worship differently. It all amounts to disrespect for the law!

This part of the story drives us to examine in ourselves and our communities how much we may feel threatened by those who do things differently or who speak or look differently. As innocent as the word may sound, difference is often not received well. In the culture and Christian religious milieu of the US, difference tends to cause fear and a sense of instability. Dislike and fear can grow into hatred. As a Christian religious community, we must be on guard against rejecting people and groups simply on the basis of their difference. In the realm of God, individuals and groups may keep their uniqueness and talents; there is room for all. We are not made to conform.

For Reflection and Discussion

1. *In sexism and anti-Judaism, women and Jews are respectively projected as other* (page 75). How does this work in your own context? When does *otherness* and difference become a threat? What groups exist in the U.S. that are projected this way? in your community? How have you experienced this *otherness?*

2. Imagine and describe Esther's feelings when she was selected and placed in the harem. How does physical beauty play a role in terms of female value today? Discuss this in terms of male/female relationships as well as female/female. Is beauty a quality that occurs often in the biblical text? In what contexts is there a mention of physical beauty in the Bible?

3. Why did Mordecai tell Esther to hide her difference? Did Esther compromise by doing this? What constituted this hiding, apart from not telling? Recall a personal experience in which being different became a hazard for yourself or someone else.

4. Read 1 Samuel 15:1-9 to refresh your memory of the history of Saul and Agag. What view do you take of Mordecai's refusal to bow down before Haman (3:2)? It could be said that he puts the life of his entire

people at risk by his stubbornness. In Chapter 3, the servants do not play an entirely sympathetic role. They "tell on" Mordecai and feed Haman's anger. Discuss possible motivations for their behavior.

5. Why does King Ahasuerus in Chapter 3 not ask for the identity of the people for whose annihilation he gives his consent? Of whom does Ahasuerus remind you?

Prayer

Dear God, teach us to hear with wide-open ears and see with wide-open eyes. Shake our stiffness, smash our desire to confine you and your Word to our ideas of what is appropriate. Help us to laugh; tickle our imagination with the stories of your wild escapades and the escapades of your people. Teach us to laugh, O God. Amen.

Chapter 2
Esther's Turn
(Esther 4–5)

In two chapters Esther is persuaded to intercede for her people (Chapter 4) and begins the process of intercession (Chapter 5). Chapter 4 is key to the unfolding of the story for in it takes place Esther's change of heart, her turnaround. Initially fearful and destabilized by Mordecai's reaction to the announced destruction of the Jews, Esther moves to a position of decision-making. In the end, she who had always done as Mordecai *charged* her (2:10, 20) now *charges* Mordecai who has to execute her orders (4:17). Almost the entire chapter consists of conversation between Mordecai and Esther, a conversation that has to be conducted via third parties. Through the conversation Esther finds a new relationship to her cousin as well as to her people.

Chapter 5 begins with Esther's first steps in the direction of intercession. Her first exchange with the king results in a party given by Esther for the king and Haman. On this occasion, the king gives her another opportunity to utter her request; and she uses this opening for an invitation to a second party (5:1-8) so that Esther's intentions remain hidden from the king and Haman. The chapter ends with a close-up of Haman in the bosom of his family (5:9-14). The result of Haman's family visit is the plan to erect a gallows for Mordecai, who will thus be executed ahead of his people. At the end of Chapter 5, the main problem is still unresolved, a new problem has been created, and readers are left in suspense as to what will come next.

A Great Lamentation
Esther 4:1-4

1. Mordecai got to know all that had been done; and Mordecai tore his clothes and dressed in sack and ashes. He went out through the city and cried a loud and bitter cry. 2. He went to the entrance of Kingsgate for no one might enter Kingsgate dressed in a sack. 3. And in province after province, wherever the king's command and his decree were announced, there was great mourning among the Jews and fasting and weeping and lamenting; sack and ashes were the bed of many.

4. Then came Esther's maids and her eunuchs and they told her. And the queen became very frightened, and she sent clothes to dress Mordecai to put aside his sack; but he would not accept.

Short units show each character taking a turn at being at the center. First Mordecai is in focus (verses 1-2) as he makes a commotion as close to the harem as he can get, while still conforming to decreed custom. We assume that the uproar is for the purpose of attracting Esther's attention. At the same time, Mordecai's lamentation is a part of a communal outbreak of grief at the impending doom of the Jews: *sack and ashes were the bed of many* (verse 3). Mordecai, bound to his people in distress and disaster to come, stands at the border between his place and Esther's place. Between him and Esther is Kingsgate. Esther's place is the harem, where they wear no sackcloth and the doom of the Jews is not known.

As the chapter opens, the public place that is the city and the province are filled with loud cries of despair; on the other side of Kingsgate lies the harem where Esther lives both a hidden, therefore protected, and at the same time isolated life. By standing at the border of the two places, Mordecai attempts to break through Esther's isolation and to draw her into a renewed connection with the very people whose association with her she has hidden up until now— by Mordecai's own request.

The Jews reportedly engage in mourning as well as fasting in anticipation of the day of their destruction, while they cry out their distress and wear symbols of mourning and repentance, sack and ashes. Fasting and wearing symbols of humility may accompany mourning and repentance (2 Kings 18:37; Ezra 8:21, 23; Nehemiah 9:1; Jonah 3:8). Traditionally, prayer would be a part of such rites; but here the mention of prayer is missing. Mordecai's *loud and bitter cry* (verse 1) is not identified as prayer, and neither are the Jews said to pray. Our attention is drawn to the omission of a religious custom at a point where one would expect it in the story. The avoidance of any mention of a religious aspect seems here to be deliberate.

If the goal of Mordecai's uproar is to draw the attention of Queen Esther, it works. She gets to hear of it via her maids and eunuchs and *became very frightened* (verse 4). One wonders about Esther's reaction. Is she afraid that Mordecai's connection with her will become public? Is she concerned about Mordecai's welfare? Has she heard about his defiance of Haman, and does she take Mordecai's clamor to mean that Haman has taken a personal revenge on him? The story reveals much and at the same time leaves many questions unanswered. If Esther is concerned about Mordecai, then why does she not ask him what is going on in the first place? The episode gives a strong impression of the extent of Esther's isolation. She, the queen of this kingdom, does not know what all the kingdom knows. Esther is a queen in name only; she does not even have the power of access to public information that belongs to every common citizen. From Chapter 3, one knows exactly how public the information is regarding the Jews. Did Esther's servants know of both the threat of annihilation of the Jews as well as Esther's nationality? Have they protected Esther by not telling her what is happening?

Esther, who was absent from the story in Chapter 3, re-enters the narrative as a frightened person. It could be that her fear is due to an instability at the core of her life: the fact that she has to keep her identity a secret. Perhaps Esther has gone around for a long time in fear of being found out. Certainly, this person in fear does not raise our expectations in terms of a role she may have to play in subsequent events.

Esther Refuses

Esther 4:5-12

5. And Esther called Hathach, a royal eunuch appointed to her, and charged him on account of Mordecai to find out what this was all about. 6. Hathach went out to Mordecai, to the city square that was in front of Kingsgate. 7. And Mordecai told him all that befell him, and also the sum of money that Haman had said to pay into the king's coffers, for the Jews, for their destruction. 8. Also, the copy of the written decree issued in Susa for their destruction he gave to him to show to Esther; and to tell her, and to charge her to go to the king, to implore and beseech him on account of her people.

9. Hathach came and told Esther Mordecai's words. 10. Esther said to Hathach and charged him to tell Mordecai: 11. "All the servants of the king and the people in the royal provinces know that if anyone, man or woman, enters the royal courtyard without an invitation, one law applies: they are killed unless the king stretches out his scepter of gold to them; then they live. As for me, I have not been invited to enter the king's presence for these thirty days." 12. So they told Mordecai Esther's words.

After Mordecai's refusal to accept the clothes, Esther sends a messenger, Hathach, to ask for information; and Hathach carries the conversation between Esther and Mordecai back and forth. Until verse 10, the dialogue remains indirect. We are told that Mordecai gives Hathach the news of the evil fate that is about to befall the Jews on his account, offering Hathach a copy of the royal decree as proof. Mordeai does this in order that Esther may see and know, so that she will be determined to mediate on behalf of her people. The verbs in verse 8 are piled up on one another: *to show . . . to tell . . . to charge . . . to go . . . to implore . . . to beseech.* Mordecai has *charged* Esther before (2:10, 20), and she did as he told her. Will it work again?

Esther's reply to Mordecai is reported as direct speech, drawing the listener more closely into the conversation, thus deepening one's involvement with the text (verse 11). Esther's words amount to a refusal and have an ironic undertone: *All the servants of the king and the people in the provinces know* what apparently Mordecai does not know. First, it is risking death to go to the king *without an invitation* and second, she has *not been invited to enter the king's presence* for a month (verse 11). Esther's world is not Mordecai's world. Her world is close and confining; it is where the master rules in his house and where no one is to approach him without his summons. On the other hand, when he summons, one is expected to appear! Nothing is known today of the custom of stretching out a scepter to those whom the king allows life, but the symbolism is clear. The scepter represents the king's power, here the power over life and death. The second piece of the information is even more disturbing than the first. A long time has passed, five years to be exact; and Esther has moved to the background of the king's awareness. Did Mordecai not know this? Has he not been as faithful in asking after his former ward's welfare as he once was? Has he been too caught up in battles of his own?

Esther's words amount to a refusal. She lives inside the palace by the laws of the kingdom at peril of her life. As a dead diplomat she will be no good to her people. The Esther who once did all that Mordecai charged her has disappeared; it is not yet entirely clear who has taken her place, but it is certainly someone who knows her reality and is able to give it a name. Esther is a survivor, and going uninvited into the king's presence is not part of her survival plan. We note the irony of the device that where once a refusal for a queen's appearance caused her disappearance, here the absence of a desire for a queen's appearance may bear the same result.

Esther in Charge
Esther 4:13-17

13. Mordecai said to return to Esther the following reply: "Do not imagine that, because you are in the royal household, you will save your life, unlike the rest of the Jews! 14. For, if you are silent, yes silent, at this time escape and deliverance will arise for the Jews from another place; but you and your father's house will perish. And who knows if for a time like this you have come to the kingdom." 15. Esther said to return to Mordecai the following reply: 16. "Go, gather all the Jews in Susa and fast on my account. Do not eat or drink for three days, night and day. I also will fast with my maids. Then I will go to the king against the law; and if I perish, I perish." 17. Mordecai left and did according to all that Esther charged him.

Mordecai, in his reply, also quoted directly, speaks tersely and not too kindly (verses 13-14). The upshot of his words to Esther is that she will not get away with her life in any case. In reality she has only one chance at survival and that is by going to the king. Her power, if she has any power at all, lies in going, not in sitting around and waiting to be invited, waiting for what will happen to her. There is the chance that it is for such purpose that she has come to the king's court in the first place. *Who knows . . .* (verse 14)?

The question *who knows?* creates strong echoes in the biblical text. It is used elsewhere to precede a reference to the possibility of God's intervention (2 Samuel 12:22; Joel 2:14; Jonah 3:9). While this question points to the possibility of God as deliverer in other texts, here the deliverer is human. Some have suggested that there is another allusion to divine intervention in Mordecai's words *escape and deliverance will arise for the Jews from another place* (verse 14). It is tempting to find at least one religious reference in a book so devoid of them, but we should probably resist the temptation. There are several openings, especially in this chapter, for references to God or to the religious life; but the narrator avoids them. The episode is almost starkly secular. Once again, for example, there is no mention of prayer where it would be most expected, at the mention of Esther's fast.

With Esther's last reply to Mordecai, any mention of messengers is omitted; and the text quotes Esther as if she is speaking directly to Mordecai. Her first words are commands: *Go, gather. . . , fast* (verse 15). She has taken charge and issues charges. She is no longer in the position of advice taker as she was previously in relation to Mordecai and Hegai (Chapter 2), nor is she the frightened questioner of the beginning of this chapter. First she issues her commands, then she announces her decision. "The Jews in the empire are already fasting, but Esther calls a fast for a different purpose than the one of bemoaning their fate. Like a soldier preparing for battle, she will fast together with her female entourage to prepare herself for the task (Judges 20:26; 1 Samuel 14:24; 2 Chronicles 20:3). In so doing she obligates her community to join her, drawing them around her as a protective force. Symbolically, she breaks down the separation between herself and her people by asking them to fast for her. From now on, she belongs to them and they to her; their fate will be her fate. . . . Esther seeks her natural alliances. She identifies herself as a Jew and as a woman, together with other Jews and other women" (*Ezra, Nehemiah, and Esther*, by van Wijk-Bos; Westminster, 1998; page 128).

For the people of God, the Jews who are suffering, help will come indeed *from another place*. It is Esther who represents the *other place*. She, a queen, is also a powerless, isolated woman who is dependent on the whims of those around her who are more powerful than she is. Even the servants of the palace know more than she does. Her predecessor was dismissed without consideration because of a minor transgression. Esther is also, although in secret, an alien. Not only is she an alien, but she is a member of a group whose very existence is under threat of extinction. Her choices are to wait passively and in fear until someone finds out about her nationality or to take her fate and that of her people into her hands and carry it to the king. Her words *I will go to the king against the law; and if I perish, I perish* (verse 17) show the degree of Esther's turnaround. She knows who she is and where she is and what she must do. There is no more hiding now. As she embraces her identity, her self-knowledge, she embraces the knowledge of the danger of what she is about to undertake. She is ready for the consequences.

If we want to identify with Esther, we can do so at the point of her lack of overt power. Esther's assigned power, that of queen, is a sham. She is an alien in an alien environment that threatens her life. Women who speak for each other's welfare may partake of the same alien quality. Women's passivity and receptivity are acceptable qualities, but their willingness to take risks on behalf of others in full knowledge of what they are doing may be less easily accepted. The power to move out of dependence on male initiative is not easily taken, even today. By putting herself in the king's way, Esther takes the initiative in her own hands and thus takes on the power that lies in herself, not in her role as ascribed to her by her environment.

A Request Postponed

Esther 5:1-8

1. So, on the third day Esther dressed in royal robes and went to stand in the inner court of the palace opposite the palace, and the king was sitting on his royal throne in the palace opposite the door opening. 2. When the king saw Queen Esther standing in the court, she found favor in his eyes; and the king stretched to Esther the golden scepter in his hand, and Esther approached and touched the top of the scepter. 3. The king said to her: "What is it, Queen Esther? What is your request? Up to half of the kingdom. . . . and it will be given to you." 4. Esther replied: "If it seems good to the king, let the king and Haman come to the party that I have prepared for them." 5. The king said for Haman to make haste to do Esther's bidding, and the king and Haman came to the party that Esther had prepared. 6. And the king said to Esther, as they were drinking the wine, "What are you asking? It will be given you, and what is your request? Even if half of the kingdom, it will be done." 7. Then Esther answered, and said: "I ask and request 8. if I have found favor in the eyes of the king, and if it seems good to the king to grant what I ask and to do according to my request: Let the king and Haman come to the party that I will prepare for them and tomorrow I will do the king's bidding."

This chapter can be divided into two main sections. In the first section, the focus is on Esther as she stands outside in the court and issues her invitation to the king. The picture is a closeup with precise positioning of the two characters: Ahasuerus inside, Esther outside within sight of the king. Very quickly the tension, raised by the end of the previous chapter, is resolved; and one knows that Esther's life is safe, for the moment at least. She has not waited the full three days of the fast but has gone to the king while the fast is still in progress. The protection of her community, symbolically present to her in the communal fast, is still with her as she stands waiting for the decision of the king.

Esther is dressed in her Sunday best, her *royal robes* (verse 1), as she stands waiting to be noticed. The king is surrounded by symbols of his authority: *the palace, the royal throne, the golden scepter* (verses 1-2). As once the lavish decorations of his palace (Chapter 1) served to *show* his splendor and greatness, the royal accouterments here point to his very real power over life and death. Vis-à-vis this power Esther stands quietly waiting for the king to make his first move. Luckily, the king must have been in a good mood; for when he sees her, *she found favor in his eyes* (verse 2). Once again, Esther has won over the male in her presence as she did when she first appeared in the royal precincts (2:9, 15, 17).

The king's generosity shows when he offers Esther as much as *half of the kingdom* (verse 3). This offer, though it should not be taken literally, indicates that he is willing to go to great lengths to satisfy Esther's desires. Esther's reply is somewhat of a surprise. Instead of pleading for the king's intervention in the fate of her people, she issues a party invitation (verse 4). Esther has learned prudence as well as independence. She knows that certain matters must be discussed only under the right circumstances. She also knows how much the king likes a good party and will use his fondness for food and wine to her advantage. Moreover, she invites also the king's most trusted advisor, Haman.

It seems anticlimactic when the tensions and expectations have risen so high, when Esther's very life is at stake, that it all would result in another party. We know already that parties in this kingdom have their very serious side, however. Important decisions can be made in the context of a party. The king, never one to pass up the opportunity to party, is willing to play along and responds with alacrity, telling Haman to *make haste to do Esther's bidding* (verse 5). The arch enemy of Esther's people is admonished by the king to follow the orders of one of his intended victims who is moreover planning to undo his schemes.

Esther has cloaked herself in more than in her royal robes; she is hiding herself and her true purpose within the traditional and acceptable role of hostess. At the party itself, she issues a second invitation when the king asks her once more what it is she wants. Her request is phrased even more politely than the first time: *I ask and request if I have found favor . . . if it seems good to the king* (verses 7-8). The elaborate polite phrase after the word *request* strings out the expectation raised by that word. Is she going to ask or is she not? Apparently, she needs more time to lay the groundwork and so asks both men to repeat the festivities the next day. What may seem like dawdling or a failure of courage, in fact, is a sure way to engage the king's attention more deeply. Now his curiosity must really be piqued, and he is sure to be all ears the next day.

Esther moves toward her goal slowly and with deliberation. The first dinner gives her the opportunity to gauge the mood of the king. She will also become better acquainted with Haman and raise the level of his confidence of which we will see evidence shortly. The purpose of Esther's parties, in contrast to those given by the king, are not to *show* herself but rather to gain life for her people. This true purpose she hides, even as her own identity is hidden from the king and Haman.

The tempo of the story has slowed almost to a standstill. The tension is kept alive only because we know that Esther will be together with the king and Haman for another entertainment. In the meantime, there is opportunity for some diversion before the big moment arrives when Esther will mediate for her people with the king.

Taking a close look at Esther's actions in this episode, it is all too easy to shrug off her efforts as those of a woman who does what women have always done. She pleases and manipulates a man by her looks and by catering to his stomach. We need to remember her lonely vigil in the courtyard, which might as easily have led to her death as to a dinner party. She, who had not been invited into the presence of the king, issues an invitation of her own. The tables are turned. She is sitting down with her oppressor and adversary: the one so gullible that he does not even know he has condemned his own queen to die; the other with such an inflated self-image that it does not occur to him that by accepting Esther's invitation he is taking the first steps on the road to his downfall. Esther gained independence and maturity during her interchange with Mordecai; but her independence is, of course, not total. She is dependent on her environment as we all are to an extent. She has wrested the initiative to her side and in such a way that no one suspects what she has in mind. The context into which she will put her request is traditional, a dinner party for her husband and trusted friend. She can only manipulate her environment to her advantage; she cannot overturn it.

To move out of passivity and take the initiative is painful and risky. We risk the death of our old selves and face the pain of seeing our environment change. Things are not the same; the old authorities are losing power, and this loss is painful. Women face these changes when they confront patriarchy while they are at table with their oppressor and adversary.

Haman at Home

Esther 5:9-14

9. And Haman went out that day happy and feeling good. And when Haman saw Mordecai at Kingsgate, who did not arise and did not move on his account, Haman was filled with fury because of Mordecai. 10. And Haman restrained himself and went home. And he sent for his friends and also his wife, Zeresh. 11. Haman told them the glory of his riches, his many children and all in which the king had made him great and had elevated him above the princes and the royal servants. 12. Haman said: "Moreover, Queen Esther let no one come together with the king to the feast she had prepared but myself; and also tomorrow I am invited together with the king. 13. And all this is nothing to me every time I see Mordecai the Jew sitting in Kingsgate." 14. His wife Zeresh, together with all his friends, said to him: "Let a gallows be erected of fifty cubits high and in the morning speak to the king, and they will hang Mordecai from it. Then go happy with the king to the party." This counsel seemed good to Haman, and he had the gallows made.

A humorous interlude with dark undertones pictures Haman on his way home and then in conversation with his family. Haman is riding high. Everything is going his way. One invitation from the queen after another, all the honors he has received—there is no end to his glory. No surprise that he is *happy and feeling good* (verse 9). Once before in the story the state of *feeling good* preceded an act of rebellion and hence was followed by uncontrollable anger (1:10-12). Here too, when Haman sees Mordecai not lying with his face in the dust before him, not making a single move in his direction as he was commanded to do, his happiness turns to rage: *Haman was filled with fury* (compare 1:12; 3:5). This time, however, he controls himself and goes home to vent his feelings.

First, Haman has a boasting session with family and friends; and they do not see at all what is keeping Haman from taking care of this little matter right away. If Haman is indeed riding so high, then no one will dare to object to the speedy demise of Mordecai, will they? In fact, why has he not thought of this before? It will be an appropriate example and show that he really means business. Mordecai, who would not *move* before Haman, will be moved to be hanged from a gallows in order to make him permanently immobile. The traditional translations have *gallows* where the Hebrew literally has *a tree*. The normal form of punishment in Persia for political offenders was impalement, but the verb used here is *hang*. In agreement with much exaggeration in the story elsewhere, the height of the gallows is outrageous: 75 feet. Haman thinks this is an excellent suggestion, and he has it looked after right away. He can always get the king's permission later.

Compare the two figures at the center of each episode. One, the woman, is at the mercy of a king and his mercurial temper. The fate of Queen Vashti would loom large over any subsequent royal consort. The reader knows that she is an alien, specifically a Jew, and is even more powerless than it may seem on the surface. Her title of queen is meaningless. The other, a man, is at the height of his power. His influence over the king is enormous, and this influence seems to be extending to the queen. He is a man of substance; he has his community, his family, and his friends at his disposal to listen to him and to give him advice. Esther, on the other hand, is entirely alone and has only the symbolic power of her community around her. She has to make up her own guidelines and has no one to advise her. Haman seems an unstoppable force of evil, Esther a helpless force for good.

It is in the figure of Esther that we may look for signs of God's presence. Rather than a God who hides in the shadows to come to the rescue with miraculous interventions, here is a God who is visible in weakness, the weakness of Esther. Esther and Haman are each on their way to determine the fate of a people. Haman is on the way to their destruction, Esther to their salvation.

Are we prepared to accept the possibility of God being present to us in those who are weak? Weakness is not a virtue in American culture. Yet, we believe that God was manifest in Jesus who showed God in the image of a servant. Can we think of how the disempowered today show us the presence of God? It is easier to admire the Hamans of this world, the men filled with purpose and their instruments of destruction, than it is to look to the Esthers who stand in the shadow, just outside the door. Yet, it is not Haman who will carry the day. Haman is like Goliath and, like Goliath, he does not see the doom that is speeding toward him because it hides in someone insignificant (1 Samuel 17).

For Reflection and Discussion

1. There are opportunities in these chapters for dramatic presentation. At least read the text aloud in the group. Form a picture of the palace complex; it does not have to be accurate. Remember that the palace was not a single building but a complex of buildings and very large. Esther must have felt small and alone standing outside the door of what was perhaps an audience room.

2. Explore the question of Esther's agitation on hearing of Mordecai's uproar (4:1 and following). Is she afraid for herself or for Mordecai? Esther is the hero of the story, the redeemer who takes responsibility for the life of her people. She is also very human with human weaknesses. We need to acknowledge her in her full humanity, including her weakness, and let her become real to us.

3. Lack of information means lack of power. Think of examples in our world where this lack becomes clear. Is it also possible that Esther has found a kind of protection in her isolation in the harem and that she is pretending not to know what is public knowledge? Esther must have felt herself to be in a weak position because she had not been invited into the king's presence for a month. She is one who has to wait on someone else's initiative before she can move. Are there connections in your own life with this type of situation?

4. If Esther has any power, it is the power of her relationship to the king. This kind of power is familiar to contemporary women. Explore some of the problems and implications of this kind of power and its uses. What alternatives are available for women today? Do you feel that Esther had an alternative? Do you think that women in general should be satisfied with the power of personal relationships?

5. Esther's royal robes in Chapter 5 are not a sign of her power, but they may provide her with a sense of confidence. Clothes sometimes give us this kind of confidence when we are about to do something difficult. "Best clothes" may be symbolic of gallantry. Think of how Ruth went to the threshing floor in her finery. Do you see other points of comparison or contrast between the Ruth and Esther story at this stage?

6. The phrase *feeling good* in both Esther and Ruth means the equivalent of having drunk too much. This drinking in Esther is often followed by anger. Anger and alcohol are intimate companions. Reflect on this connection as you have experienced it.

7. Haman stands in stark contrast to Esther in all respects. Apart from being powerful, he is also ridiculous and boastful. His speech to his wife and friends sounds funny. What other parts of these chapters can be seen as humorous? Is it difficult to accept humor in the Bible? Do you know other biblical stories that can be perceived as humorous?

Prayer

Loving, protecting God, we are often ruled by fear. Fear of what others will think of us, fear of what the future will bring, fear of death. With Esther, help us to step out of the shadows of our fear. Give us the courage to claim ourselves as your children and to claim life for those who are outside the house of royal privilege. Give us the sureness of Esther that we may not be intimidated by those in power and stand before them knowing that your strength is perfected in weakness. Give us hope that a better day will dawn when love of kindness and pursuit of justice will be a surer sign of strength than love of weaponry. Make this day come soon, O God, for the sake of the victims of war and violence; we pray in Jesus' name. Amen.

CHAPTER 3

HAMAN'S DOWNFALL

(ESTHER 6–7)

BEFORE WE HEAR THE REVELATION OF ESTHER'S REQUEST TO THE KING, there is another humorous interlude with dark undertones that foreshadow the actual downfall of Haman. In Chapter 6, Esther has entirely disappeared from the scene; and the action is between the king, his advisor Haman, and Mordecai. The king, on having the daily records read to him, discovers the good turn Mordecai once did him and, on finding out he was never rewarded for his role in the affair, wants to make up for the oversight (6:1-3). As usual, he seeks advice in figuring out how to go about things; and who better to ask than Haman, who is around the court anyway. When the king asks Haman what he thinks should be done to honor someone who deserves honor from the king, the reader is informed that Haman applies the king's intentions to himself; and so Haman goes to outrageous lengths in his suggestions for honoring this individual (6:4-9). When this person turns out to be Mordecai, Haman must do as he himself had instructed. The irony of Mordecai's elevation at the cost of Haman's humiliation is not lost on the reader and is also a portent of Haman's greater fall to come (4:10-12). Once again at home, Haman's family is as eager to warn him of possible impending doom as they were once ready to encourage him to destroy the person who beclouded his happiness (4:13-14).

Chapter 7 recounts the second party of Esther for the king and Haman and Esther's intervention on behalf of her people and accusation of Haman. This time, when the king asks Esther what it is she desires, Esther asks for her own life and the life of her people, including in her request an implied accusation that someone is involved in the impending destruction (7:3-4). The accusation naturally leads to the king's question about the identity of the perpetrator, and Esther points to Haman (7:5-6). While the king takes a walk in the garden, Haman throws himself on Esther's mercy, a move that is interpreted by the king, when he returns at the right moment, as intended rape (7:7-8). Then Haman's fate is sealed. On a eunuch's advice, Haman is hanged from the gallows he has erected for Mordecai, thus neatly walking into the trap he has set for another.

Mordecai's Elevation
Esther 6

1. That same night sleep fled the king, and he said to bring the book of the records of daily affairs; and they were read in the presence of the king. 2. And it was found written that Mordecai had told of Bigthana and Teresh, the two royal eunuchs, guardians of the threshold, who had sought to lay hands on King Ahasuerus. 3. And the king said: "What was done to honor and exalt Mordecai because of this?" And the young men who were serving the king said: "Nothing was done for him." 4. The king said: "Who is in the court?" Now Haman had entered the palace outer court to tell the king to hang Mordecai on the gallows erected for him. 5. And the young men of the king said to him: "Look, there is Haman standing in the court." And the king said: "Let him enter." 6. And Haman came in, and the king said to him: "What should be done for the man whom the king delights in honoring?" Haman said to himself: "Whom would it delight the king to honor except myself?" 7. And Haman said to the king: "As far as the man whom it delights the king to honor: 8. Let them bring a royal robe worn by the king and a horse ridden by the king, on whose head a royal crown is placed. 9. Let the robe and the horse be given into the care of one of the king's most noble princes; then let him clothe the man whom it delights the king to honor, and lead him on horseback through the city-square; and let him call out before him: 'Thus it will be done to the man whom it delights the king to honor!' " 10. And the king said to Haman: "Quick, take the robe and the horse of which you spoke and do thus to Mordecai, the Jew who customarily sits in Kingsgate; do not leave anything you said undone!" 11. And Haman took the robe and the horse, dressed Mordecai, and guided him on horseback through the city-square, calling out before him: "Thus it will be done to the man whom it delights the king to honor!"

12. And Mordecai returned to Kingsgate, and Haman hastened to his house in mourning with his head covered. 13. Haman recounted to Zeresh, his wife, and to all his friends all that had befallen him. And his counselors and Zeresh, his wife, said to him: "If Mordecai, before whom you have begun to fall, is Jewish, then you will not best him but you will fall, yes fall, before him." 14. While they were yet speaking with him, the royal eunuchs approached to bring him hastily to the party that Esther had prepared.

From one home, Haman's house, the story moves to another, the king's palace, where the king is having a sleepless night. Perhaps from having eaten and drunk too well, the king is not able to sleep and has the daily records read to him. Thus it comes to the attention of Ahasuerus that Mordecai once saved his life. On his question as to what was done to reward Mordecai, the plain truth is *nothing* (verse 3), a truth provided by a group of servants. Something must be done, according to the king; but as ever he cannot accomplish his intentions without advice. He asks whether anyone is around. The narrator informs the reader, before the servants can say anything, that Haman is around, including the reason for his nocturnal visit (verse 4). He has come because he is out to get Mordecai as soon as possible. His purpose and that of his king run counter to one another, but neither one of them knows about this. The servants point out Haman to the king, who decides to consult him; for who could be more suitable to help Ahasuerus in a delicate matter of this sort than his most trusted advisor (verse 5)?

A delightful conversation follows (verses 6-9). It is delightful because of the cross purposes of the king and Haman and because the reader is let in on the joke. As soon as the king begins talking about the man whom the king delights in honoring (verse 6), Haman can think of no one but himself. His directions are very precise and designed to deliver a psychological blow to those who might compete with him for the king's favor. The princes who are most noble will be the very ones to dress him and to lead him around on horseback, crying out as town-criers do: "*Thus it will be done. . . .*" (verse 9).

To wear a robe that the king had worn and to ride a horse that the king had ridden would in themselves be marks of the highest honor, but as usual Haman does not know where to stop. So he adds delightful touches, touches that involve put-downs for other contenders for the king's favor. Alas, he does not know that with every word he increases his own impending humiliation. As once he hid from the king the identity of those he had earmarked for destruction, so the king hides from Haman the identity of the one he intends to honor.

Haman's advice pleases the king, who instructs him to take care of everything (verse 10). As soon as the king uttered his first words, Haman must have known that things were not going as expected; and then the name of the honoree sounded, *Mordecai*. **Mordecai**? There must be some mistake! But, just in case, and so there is no cause for misunderstanding, the king identifies the man even more closely as *the Jew who customarily sits in Kingsgate* (verse 10). There is no way out for Haman. He must do as the king commands. And so, perhaps with his mouth still hanging open, he assists Mordecai in dressing and guides him around on the horse. Mordecai, who would not bow before Haman, is now elevated above him; and Haman must announce the honor done to Mordecai and act as a servant to this despised man. This role reversal bodes ill for Haman. He hurries home to talk about his misfortune *in mourning with his head covered* (verse 12), in total contrast to his earlier return home (5:9).

In this episode, Haman and the king compete for obtuseness. The darkness of the night may be seen as symbolic for their lack of insight. Haman is blinded to anyone's virtues but his own. The king who had forgotten Mordecai's service of which he had once been clearly informed (2:22), refers to Mordecai as a Jew without making the connection between him and the community he has doomed to extinction not so long ago. Ahasuerus seems incapable of thinking or acting for himself; his part of the conversation consists mostly of the questions *what, who,* and *how*. Haman is ready with advice, but he can only think of himself and his importance; so he overreaches himself.

This time, as he arrives at home, his friends and family do not cheer up Haman. They believe that this is the beginning of the end and announce this to Haman in no uncertain terms. Although no one yet suspects Esther of having a hand in Haman's collapse, as she indeed has been absent from the previous scene, family and friends ascribe the impending doom to Jewish superiority. Haman's community sounds as if it has already given him up for dead. We notice the emphatic use of the verb *fall* in verse 13. *You have begun to fall. . . , you will fall, yes fall. . . .* For Haman the events are taking a downward turn. As Esther did, he hung around the court; but unlike Esther, he was in the wrong place at the wrong time. In the meantime, there is a gallows waiting for someone.

The episode does not itself advance the plot; if Mordecai had not been elevated, and Haman not been humiliated, this would not have changed events to come. Nothing has been solved by Mordecai's being honored; the fate of his people still hangs in the balance. For the most part then, the episode provides entertainment and prepares the ground more thoroughly for Haman's ultimate undoing, which is about to happen. At the point that his ego is at its most inflated, the balloon is pricked by none other than the king himself; and he has to eat humble pie! To top it all off, his own wife utters words of the direst warning. The events and conversation described provide the reader with some much relished anticipation for the collapse of the villain of the piece.

At Table With Esther

Esther 7:1-8

1. The king and Haman came to feast with Queen Esther. 2. On the second day, as they were drinking the wine, the king said again to Esther: "What are you asking, Queen Esther? It will be given to you. What do you request? Even if half of the kingdom, it will be done." 3. Then Queen Esther replied and said: "If I have found favor in your eyes, O king, and if it seems good to the king, let my life be given to me on my asking, and my people on my request. 4. For we have been sold, I and my people, for destruction, for slaughter and annihilation; if we were to be sold as servants and maids, I would have been silent, but there is no adversary worth the injury to the king." 5. Then King Ahasuerus said to Queen Esther: "Who is this and where is he who has set his heart on this?" 6. Esther replied: "An enemy and adversary, this wicked Haman here!" Then Haman was in terror before the king and the queen. 7. And the king arose in his fury from the feast and went into the garden court while Haman stood ready to beg his life from Queen Esther for he saw that nothing good would come to him from the king. 8. And the king returned from the garden court to the banquet hall just as Haman was falling on the couch where Esther lay. And the king said: "Would he even ravish the queen with me present in the house?" As soon as the words left the mouth of the king, they covered Haman's face.

Events now hasten to a conclusion. We find the king and Haman at the second party given by the queen; and as the king repeats his question to

Esther for the third time, she finally speaks her request. After the introductory, etiquette-required phrases, she immediately states her business: *Let my life be given . . .* (verse 3). She asks for her own life first, not perhaps so much out of self-interest, but because the life of her people depends on her. Also, the king's interest is in her. She says as much as, "It's about my life, yes, and that of my whole people!" Then she repeats the life-threatening situation with the same words that were used in the announcement of the decree: destruction, slaughter, and annihilation (3:13). The next phrase is a disclaimer that she would not have bothered with this request if it had been a lesser matter than one of life and death. The last words of verse 4 are difficult to translate but introduce the word *adversary*, which provides the opening for the king to ask his question about the identity of the villain who is behind this scheme. And Esther, without further ado, points to Haman who is rightly terrified by these developments.

Let my life be given to me. . . . She could have said, "Have Haman killed and undo the decree issued in regard to the Jews." She could have said many things. Instead her request is simple and goes straight to the heart of the matter. Nothing less than life is at stake. And her life and that of her people are interwoven. She speaks exactly the right words to make the king ask who is responsible. The question from the king then provides her with the opening to point the finger at Haman. The exchange between the king and the queen is almost rhythmic:

Who is this and where is he . . . (verse 5)?
An enemy and adversary, this wicked Haman here! (verse 6)

Although the king too was responsible, Esther manages to separate him from Haman in her reply. We note that the identity of the culprit may be clear to the king but not the identity of the people to whom Esther is referring. She calls them here *my people* rather than *the Jews* (verse 3). That she names them so indicates also her embracing of her community as her own. In choosing for her own life at this crucial moment, she chooses at the same time for her community.

The whole thing throws the king into a proper quandary. He is good mostly at asking questions and getting advice. Where shall he turn for counsel now that his most trusted advisor stands exposed? It is not at all clear what the king will do, nor is it clear that Esther has achieved success. Decisions still hang in the balance. The king could decide that her word is not enough to convict Haman, that he needs to ask some other advice, or that she has overreached herself and must be punished. In any case, the whole thing puts him in a temper; and he goes to take a walk, to cool off, to think things over. It is at that moment that Haman makes his final mistake. Shaken up as he already was by the events of the previous night, not having had much sleep, after depressing counsel from his nearest and dearest, he is now truly terrified. He makes a choice between king and queen and chooses wrong. He decides to throw himself on the mercy of Queen Esther; he who would have destroyed her life and the life of her people is now ready to beg his life from her (verse 7). The king, on his return, finds Haman *falling on the couch where Esther lay* and accuses him of accosting the queen (verse 8). This is the final case of crossed signals between king and advisor. Haman's fall is almost complete. Whether the king is pretending and uses it as a handy excuse, or whether he really thinks that Haman had rape in mind, it makes no difference to the outcome. This is the end of the line for Haman. Now, Haman does not cover his own head in grief and shame, others cover it for him as a sign of his fall from favor.

Haman's Elevation

Esther 7:9-10

9. Then said Harbona, one of the eunuchs before the king: "Look, there is already a gallows, which Haman made for Mordecai, whose word saved the king, standing at Haman's house, fifty cubits high!" The king said: "Hang him on it." 10. So they hanged Haman on the gallows that he had erected for Mordecai, and the anger of the king abated.

It is obvious that Haman must die, and once more there are servants to lend a helping hand, led by the eunuch Harbona. As earlier the servants pointed out Haman as standing around when the king needed advice (6:5), now Harbona points out that there is already a gallows standing around, ready to be used. He also adds, helpfully, that Haman had intended this gallows for Mordecai, the one who had saved the king's life and who has just been honored for it (verse 9). Enough said. The king orders immediate execution.

There Haman swings from the gallows he erected for his enemy, elevated higher than he could ever have thought. He has walked straight into the trap he set for his arch enemy. A very satisfactory case of poetic justice has been concluded with this third and last punishment of an individual at the conclusion of a party.

Why did the king become so angry with Haman? Esther has no proof nor is she asked to prove anything. The king believes her on her word. His temper is quickly aroused, especially after some wine; he is gullible and easily convinced. But what exactly has Haman done wrong from the point of view of the king? If we review the situation, we can say that he asked permission to destroy an entire people, permission that the king gave readily. We assume that Haman did not know that Queen Esther was a member of this people just as the king did not know. As the king's advisor he has made a grave error, but the king himself is equally guilty of planning to murder his queen. The roles of Ahasuerus and Haman are not so easily disentangled. Perhaps that is precisely what infuriates the king, that Haman's wickedness throws light on his own involvement. It is easier to become furious with Haman than to face himself.

The tyrant is a fool, and his henchman is doomed; for no tyrant enjoys looking his own folly in the face. Yet, Haman might have made a case for himself. He did not know, after all, that Queen Esther was a Jew. It may be that his humiliation before Mordecai has killed his flair, for his choice of intercessor is fatal. In going after a woman's soft heart, he seems to be going after her body. At least, that is how the king makes it appear. There is a strong impression from the story that Haman is not much liked by anyone. His wife and friends are almost indecently quick to point to his beginning downfall (6:13); the servants point the finger at his presence during the king's sleepless night (6:5); now they make the king aware of the availability of the gallows (7:9). Haman has brought his power home to too many people, and such wielders of power are often disliked and even hated.

Esther is safe for the moment, but the fate of the Jews is not yet resolved. Yet, Haman's death gives her a much needed advantage. Now, she only has to press the advantage home. There is another advantage of which she may still be unaware. It is not clear whether she has heard of Mordecai's good fortune. One would think that the servants told her. She may indeed be keeping the information about their relationship until another moment. In any case, the royal favor received by Mordecai can only serve him and Esther well in advancing their cause.

Among many ironies, it is ironic that the one wickedness of which Haman is not guilty, that of rape, is the one that sends him to his death.

The death of Haman is anticipatory of the death of his plans. The precise undoing of them is still to come, but it is now clear that the jaws of death are ready for others than the Jews.

We remind ourselves again that although the story is not history, the situations and characters are mirrors in which we see reflections of ourselves. When we look in the mirror of Haman, whose hatred against the Jews overtook his reason and good sense, we may consider Christian intolerance and persecution of the Jews past and present. When we look in the mirror of the king, who pretended not to know anything because it was easier that way, we may contemplate our own unwillingness to be engaged, our wilful denial of injustice against individuals and groups, and our reluctance to face our own participation in such injustice. When we look in the mirror of Mordecai, who had the courage and dignity to stand up to the tyrant, we may think of the occasions when we have said no, when we have stood up against injustice even when it has seemed a trivial matter. Finally, we look in the mirror of Esther, who grew in maturity, who went alone against the law, who spoke prudently and saved the life of a people. We know that even if we have never done such a grand deed, we hope that we may find courage for ourselves to go it alone when we must, to bide our time and to lay our plans well for the survival of those who are victims of violence and injustice.

In this story, all ends well for the two who fight for the life of their people; for this is a comedy, and it is designed to lift the spirits of an oppressed and persecuted people. In history, the ones who stand alone against the forces of evil do not often come out on top. Yet, their voices sound through the ages to call later generations to their task.

Once more, we contemplate the phrase *Let my life be given to me. . . .* Who are the ones that ask for life today? Who are the ones who have the power to give life and to take it away? For Esther life means, clearly, physical survival. In the Bible, life is always more than mere existence, however. Life is existence in right relationship with God and neighbor. Jesus came, according to the Gospel of John, that we may "have life, and have it abundantly" (John 10:10).

From Esther we may learn at least one thing about life. Life involves making choices. That God is in charge of life does not mean that human beings can leave things safely up to God and go their way as if they had no role in the matter. Doing that would be the way of King Ahasuerus.

God involves us in the way of life, and we can make choices for or against it. Esther is able to make her request for life, because she has already made a choice for life when she says *I will go to the king against the law and if I perish, I perish* (4:16). When she makes that decision, she chooses for the life of her people and herself.

For Reflection and Discussion

1. Reflect on the healing power of laughter. Think of a time when laughter helped you to get through a difficult situation, sadness, or despair. In describing Abraham and Sarah's laughter, Frederick Buechner writes: "Where does their laughter come from? It comes from as deep a place as tears come from, and in a way it comes from the same place. As much as tears do, it comes out of the darkness of the world where God is of all missing persons the most missed, except that it comes not as an ally of darkness but as its adversary, not as a symptom of darkness but as its antidote." (*Telling the Truth: The Gospel as Comedy, Tragedy and Fairy Tale*, Harper and Row, 1977; page 55). Discuss this statement.

2. Esther finally makes her request. She asks for life. She had already made a choice for life when she took her fate and that of her people into her own hands. Life then involves risk and pain, even at its fullest. Life involves choices. What does "eternal life" mean in this context?

3. What do you think about Esther's behavior in Chapter 8? Should she have shown mercy to Haman? Should she have told the king that he was not molesting her? Or do you think Haman got what he deserved? What could be wrong with that line of thought? Is Haman the "fall-guy" for the king?

4. The author asks us to consider ourselves in different "mirrors" (page 105). Find other reflections in Vashti, in Haman's family, and in the servants, for example.

Prayer

Holy God, giver of life, we confess our shortsightedness, our inability to see beyond our own importance, our reluctance to face our participation in practices and patterns of destruction. Open our eyes to the love you foster for the whole creation. Give us the courage and the passion to make choices that enhance life, to take a stand against the forces of evil and on the side of those who suffer injustice. Make your love for all creation real through our lives. Amen.

Chapter 4
A People Saved
(Esther 8–10)

Esther's task is not yet done. Although Haman is destroyed, the evil he has set loose in the realm is still at large. Chapter 8 deals with the difficulty of an immutable royal edict that necessitates renewed efforts at intercession on Esther's part (8:3-8). A clever way out of the dilemma is found and communicated across the realm by the usual method (8:9-14). A final section records the reaction to the good news among the Jews (8:15-17). As once the effects of a royal proclamation upon the Jews in Persia had been mourning and lamenting (4:3), now there is *light and happiness, exultation and honor* (8:16). Chapter 9 describes the results of the permission for the Jews to defend themselves at the time of their planned annihilation (9:1-17), followed by an account of the establishing of the festival of Purim (9:18-23). The last section of Chapter 9 together with Chapter 10, which consists only of a few verses, is essentially a recapitulation of the gist of the Book of Esther and may be viewed as a kind of postscript to the story. The chapters are presented partially in translation; for other parts, consult a standard Bible translation, such as the New Revised Standard Version of the Bible.

There is some tension created in these final chapters by the assignment of a more important role to Mordecai to which Esther takes a background seat. She is still in the foreground in the opening episode of Chapter 8; but there is no mention of her in relation to the edict for the Jews, which goes out by Mordecai's hand in the name of the king (8:8-14). In Chapter 9, Esther steps to the fore once more with her request that the Jews may have an extra day to defend themselves (9:13-17); but she is gone again when the institution of Purim is ascribed to Mordecai alone (9:20-23). In the recapitulation Esther takes up her proper place as the intercessor for her people and the one who, together with Mordecai, instituted and regulated the Feast of Purim (9:24-32); but Chapter 10 reverts to putting Mordecai in the limelight. This see-sawing back and forth between the two characters leaves the reader with a sense of untidiness. As a wrap-up, these chapters are not very satisfactory. As Timothy Beal observes: "The narrative appears to be oblivious to the reader or congregation's desire for a tidier sense of an ending. The effect of this is to leave readers and hearers somewhat disoriented, restless. Like Mordecai in Chapter 2, we are left standing on the edge of this narrative world, wondering what happened to. . . ." (*Esther in Berith Olam—Studies in Hebrew Narrative and Poetry,* by Timothy K. Beal; Collegeville, Minnesota, 1999; page 118). It is possible that the shifting attention from Esther to Mordecai and back reflects the reality that there were originally two stories with two different characters in the center that were woven together in the Book of Esther.

A Task Completed

Esther 8:1-8

1. On that day King Ahasuerus gave to Queen Esther the house of Haman, the enemy of the Jews, and Mordecai came before the king, for Esther had told what he was to her. 2. The king removed his ring, which he had passed to Haman, and gave it to Mordecai. And Esther gave Mordecai charge over the house of Haman.

3. Then Esther spoke again before the king, and she fell at his feet and wept and pled with him to avert the evil of Haman, the Agagite, and his plan, which he plotted against the Jews. 4. And the king stretched out to Esther the golden scepter, and Esther arose and stood before the king. 5. And she said: "If it seems good to the king, and if I have found favor in his eyes, and if the matter seems right to the king, and if I am good in his eyes, let it be written to overturn the letters and the plan of Haman, the son of Hammedatha, the Agagite, that he wrote to destroy the Jews who are in all the provinces of the king. 6. For how can I bear and look on the evil that has found my people, and how can I bear and look on the destruction of my kindred?" 7. And King Ahasuerus said to Queen Esther and to Mordecai the Jew: "Look, Haman's house I have given to Esther and him they hanged on the gallows because he had stretched out his hand against the Jews. 8. Now you yourselves write to the Jews as is good in your eyes in the name of the king, and seal it with the king's ring, for a writing written in the name of the king and sealed with the king's ring cannot be overturned."

Two verses serve to transfer Haman's property and his authority to Esther and Mordecai. The relationship between Esther and Mordecai is now in the open; and Mordecai moves from the boundaries between palace and city, Kingsgate, to the inside of the palace, *before the king* (verse 1). The king then hands him the ring, which previously had been Haman's, to signify the transfer of Haman's authority to Mordecai. Following suit, Esther transfers the charge of Haman's house to Mordecai. From Mordecai's ward who did as *he charged her* (2:10, 19), she has become a person with enough authority that she can delegate it to others.

Yet, in the next moment we find Esther in a humble posture before the king, *she fell at his feet* (verse 3), engaged in tearful pleading on behalf of her people. There is no mention of the danger she might run even now in appearing before the king uninvited, yet she waits to speak until the king stretches out his golden scepter. The king had given her Haman's house, but her task is not completed. As is the way sometimes with a difficult task, the hardest part begins when one might think it is finished. There is a snag in the proceedings. Even though Haman is dead, the edict of the king cannot be overturned by just another edict. Another plan will have to be devised to save the Jews, and another test of Esther and Mordecai's ingenuity is about to take place. The breathtaking moments are over, the waiting in the courtyard, the decisions of when to reveal one's true intentions. Now comes the responsibility of further enlightening the king and acquiring his consent for a change in the events to come.

Esther's posture of supplication and her tears, heretofore not mentioned as a part of her intercession, underline the importance of the moment. When she speaks, her phrasing is even more elaborate and polite than it has been in the past: *if it seems good . . . if I have found favor . . . if the matter seems right . . . if I am good* (verse 5). She repeats each matter, that of the issue itself and her own person, insofar as it must please the king. I have retained the word *good*, so indicative of earlier interchanges with this mercurial monarch (1:19; 2:4; 3:9; 5:4, 8; 7:3) and of a quality designed to win people over (1:11; 2:7, 9). She asks that the decree written earlier for the destruction of the Jews may be overturned by another decree. There is an emphatic reference to Haman in her words, including his lineage. Is she trying to reassure the king that she does not hold him culpable but only Haman? It was after all a *royal* decree that had gone out against the Jews.

Esther's plea contains a threefold reference to the Jews. She calls them the *Jews* (verse 5) first, and then proceeds to identify them as *my people* and *my kindred* (verse 6), thus moving from the larger to the smaller context and the one that is of the most immediate concern. These are the Jews, but they are also *her people and her relatives!* (verse 6) Surely, it is clear that she will not be able to stand to witness their destruction. This is the first time that Esther refers to her people by name. She has now sealed the identification of herself and her community. Altogether the word *Jews* occurs with great frequency in this chapter and the next to indicate the shift in focus that is taking place from Esther and Mordecai to their people, from palace to the Jewish community.

Esther's elaborate and emphatic plea may be motivated by fear that the king at this point is not as easily interested in the whole affair. And indeed, his majesty's reply sounds somewhat wearied: *Haman's house I have given to Esther and him they hanged on the gallows. . .* (verse 7). What more is he expected to do? Thus he turns the task over to Esther and Mordecai with his permission and the seal of his authority. They will have to arrange it themselves; it is simply becoming too much for a busy monarch! *You yourselves write* (verse 8) advises the king; and think of a way to change an unchangeable decree, he might have added. For how this is to be done is by no means clear.

A Royal Reversal

Esther 8:9–9:17

9. Then the secretaries of the king were called at that time, in the third month, that is the month Sivan, on the twenty-third day; and it was written, according to all that Mordecai commanded, to the Jews and the satraps and governors and officials of the provinces from India to Ethiopia, 127 provinces, to each province in its script and each people in its language, and to the Jews according to their script and language....

15. And Mordecai went out from the presence of the king dressed in royal robes of blue and white, with a great crown of gold and a mantle of fine linen and purple; and the city of Susa shouted for happiness. 16. For the Jews there was light and happiness, exultation and honor. 17. And in every province and city, where the word of the king and his decree came, there was happiness and exultation for the Jews, a party and a holiday. And many of the natives made themselves out as Jewish for the fear of the Jews had fallen upon them.

No attention is given to any deliberation Esther and Mordecai might have had; rather, the story moves into an immediate report of the letter that was sent out, by whom it was sent, under whose authority and by what means it went out (8:9-10). Only after these facts are firmly established does the information appear as to how the Jews are to escape their fate. In language that echoes the manner of issuing the earlier edict that went out against them (3:9-14), the Jews are informed that they will be allowed to defend themselves on the day that was scheduled for their annihilation; indeed, they will thus be able to turn the tables and perpetrate on their adversaries what they had planned to do to them: *to destroy, to kill and to annihilate* (verse 11).

From verse 9 in Chapter 8 through the first part of the next chapter, Mordecai is in the center. It is by his hand that the new edict goes out (verses 9-10), and it is his appearance that causes the city of Susa to rejoice. Esther has disappeared into the background of the tale, although she will reappear. From now on Mordecai and Esther take turns being in the center of attention.

The tone of 8:15-17 is heavily ironic. Everything is reversed. The person once in sack and ashes, not allowed to come closer to the palace than Kingsgate (4:1-2), now comes out of the palace dressed in royal finery. While at the edict against the Jews the city of Susa was thrown *in confusion* (3:15), now it *shouted for happiness* (8:15). The Jews for whom once sack and ashes served as couches now exist in a cloud of happiness (verse 16). The word *happiness*, until now reserved for the enemy of the Jews (5:9, 14), is here applied to the city and the Jews themselves. The greatest irony is embedded in the announcement that many natives tried to pass for Jews (verse 17). The verb used occurs only here in the Bible and is made up for the purpose; literally, the text states that the Persians were *Jewing*. It is not clear what exactly would constitute such a charade; and we are free to let our imagination play with the image of putting on things to wear, imitating accents, eating certain dishes, just to make sure no one would suspect they were Gentiles! In terms of the Hitler years in Europe, here everyone is anxiously cutting a yellow star to sew on their clothes.

The role reversal is total, to the extent that *the fear of the Jews had fallen upon them.* Realistically speaking, nothing here makes much sense. Why would a Persian city rejoice in the potential victory of the Jewish community? Why would the Jews be so happy before they know how things will fall out? Why would the Jews inspire fear since they posed hardly a threat as a small minority among many other minorities, scattered throughout the kingdom in the vast Persian realm? There is a sense of poking fun here, both at the former enemy, delirious with joy, and at the Jews themselves. They are so sure of a victory that they are already on cloud nine, months ahead of time, while everyone cowers before them in fear and tries to join their ranks. The reversal is complete on the day that the former victims become warriors, *the day that the enemies of the Jews had hoped to gain mastery over them, that day was turned around, and the Jews gained mastery over their foes* (9:1).

Without further descriptions, the narrative jumps to the twelfth of Adar, when reportedly the Jews strike their enemies without any opposition (9:1-10). This makes the king very happy, and he voluntarily provides Esther with a last opportunity to make a demand (9:11-17). There is a negative and unfunny side to the reversal of victims and oppressors as well. One of the most devastating results of violence and oppression is that it may set off counter-violence. The oppressed then turn into a mirror image of the former oppressor. Thus, the greatest evil produced by those who engage in violence may well be a lasting hatred on the part of their victims. In the story of Esther, exactly such destruction now befalls the population of Persia (9:1-16). The most disconcerting moment in the book comes when Esther, as her last request, asks for the violence now perpetrated by the Jews to go on for another day. In addition, Esther asks for the death of Haman's sons.

This very last request of Esther may seem redundant, since Haman's sons were reportedly killed already (9:7-9). It may also be that we discern here the seam where two stories were woven together, one with Mordecai in the center and one with Esther. The focus in these chapters moves from Esther to Mordecai and back again, with some duplicate material present as the killing of Haman's sons and the writing of the letter that institutes Purim (9:20 and 29).

The comic note returns with the report of the king's satisfaction over the demise of so many of his subjects. We may imagine him rubbing his hands together in satisfaction, exclaiming that if it was this well done in the city, how good must it have been in the provinces (9:11-12)! It is hard to picture a "real" king, even a foolish one, taking this attitude toward his own people.

A People's Feast
Esther 9:18-23

18. And the Jews who were in Susa gathered on the thirteenth day and on the fourteenth, and rested on the fifteenth and made it a day of parties and happiness. 19. Therefore the Jews of the villages who live in open towns hold the fourteenth day of the month of Adar as a day for happiness and parties, a holiday, a sending of gifts of food to one another.

Gradually the attention shifts toward the celebration of Purim, the celebration of Jewish survival. In this section and the next, the holiday is marked by gifts, both to one's neighbor and to the poor (verse 22). In this connection, we observe also that the story reports three times that the Jews took no property *they did not touch the plunder* (9:10, 15, 16). This abstinence is in contrast to the plunder that would have been allowed to their foes (3:13). Purim is a feast of triumph and also of generosity, and the practices of Purim are not for revenge on an enemy. The customs of the festival at this point guide the story, and it may be that Esther's request for a second day of self-defense is demanded by conflicting dates regarding the institution of Purim.

All of the excessive and unbelievable facets of the story as related in Chapters 8 and 9 may be assigned to the character of Purim. Purim is a feast that partakes of burlesque and carnival; people dress up outlandishly and play roles. The rules may be broken at Purim; and the story of Esther breaks all the rules of propriety and moderation, of religiosity even and piety. Esther is not historical reporting but a Br'er Rabbit story that turns everything on its head: Mighty kings are depicted as blind fools. Wicked tyrants overreach themselves and walk into the trap they set for others. A member of a despised minority slated for destruction is elevated by royal honor and glory. A foreign woman bound by the limitations of her sex, her nationality, and the customs of the harem saves the day not just for herself but for her entire people. Finally, this people turns into a mighty warrior tribe on the very day that their victimization was to be completed.

This final party, the party of survival, this people's celebration, needs to be seen in contrast to the opening party of King Ahasuerus. The opening party went on too long, splendor and ostentation were at thc center, and the party ended in an outrageous punishment of a small act of rebellion. The last party, *Purim*, begins in bloodshed. Yet, this party, unlike that of the first chapter, is one of people with each other. People give gifts; those who are not well-off especially benefit (9:22). On a woman's intercession and by a woman's guidance, the customs of Purim were established. A woman would not come into the king's presence when invited, and disaster occurred. A woman came to the king uninvited, and events took a turn so that the tale ends with sounds of laughter and the fireworks of rejoicing.

The Salient Facts

Esther 9:24–10:3

24. For Haman, the son of Hammedatha, the Agagite, the enemy of all the Jews, had planned against the Jews to destroy them; and he cast Pur, that is the lot, to crush and destroy them. 25. When she came before the king, he said in a letter to turn around his evil plan he had planned against the Jews on his own head; and they hanged him and his sons on the gallows. 26. Therefore these days are called Purim, after the name Pur.

The end of Chapter 9 sums up the salient facts of the story of Esther. In the matter of the royal letter that overturned the earlier decree against the Jews, Mordecai is not mentioned at all, as if the king without his or Esther's help took care of turning Haman's plans around. Many translations insert Esther in verse 25, *when Esther came before the king*. . . . It is clear enough that Esther is meant, but it may be important to stay close to the Hebrew in this case. When a pronoun is used without its antecedent, it may be to attract attention to the person. Who is this *she*? She is the woman, the alien, the orphan, the queen without royal power, the uninvited woman in the harem, the one who hid her identity, Esther. The one without power approached the one with all the power, the *he* mentioned in the next phrase. The use of the pronoun *he* in verse 25 is worth attention also. Only if one knows what went before is it clear that there are two different *he's* involved in the sentence. In addition, common sense would dictate there are two different subjects since it is difficult to imagine anyone ordering his own demise. First, *he said* indicates the king; then, with the possessive pronoun *his* the reference changes to Haman, to stay there throughout the rest of the verse. The two *he's* are as entangled in the sentence as they were collaborators in the plan to destroy the Jews.

The word *plan* occurs repeatedly in this short section. *Plan* stands in contrast to *pur*, the lot, chance. Haman's *plans* come to naught; they were tied in with chance. Esther counterplanned evil of Haman. The feast that resulted is called *Purim*, the feast of chance. Yet, it was not chance that saved the people but Esther's clever and timely intercession with the help of Mordecai. How and where God is involved with Esther's efforts is left to the imagination of the readers or to their faith.

The very last verses of Chapter 9 form a contrast both to an earlier section (9:20-23) and to Chapter 10. Here Esther is in the center of establishing and organizing Purim with Mordecai at her side:

29. And Queen Esther, the daughter of Abihail, wrote together with Mordecai, the Jew, with all authority to ratify this second letter concerning Purim. 30. She sent letters to all the Jews in the 127 provinces of Ahasuerus's kingdom with words of peace and truth: 31. to fix the days of this Purim on the proper dates as Mordecai the Jew fixed it for them and Esther the queen, just as they had fixed for themselves and their descendants practices of fasting and lamenting. 32. So Esther's word fixed these practices of Purim, and it was preserved in writing.

Is this an alternative account to the earlier report of Mordecai's letter to institute Purim? Or is it intended as a follow-up to Mordecai's earlier instructions, this time with Esther's authority added? It is not clear. These last chapters create some tension in terms of assigning more authority to Mordecai and a bigger role in the scheme of things at the cost of depriving Esther of her central place. If two original stories were woven together, this part of the text might represent a lack of success in combining the two roles in the aftermath of the story. In the actual story, Mordecai and Haman are foils for each other. Mordecai sets Haman's vindictiveness in motion and shows up his arrogance and self-aggrandizement. The Haman-Mordecai encounters form subplots to the main plot, the development and undoing of a threat to the life of the Jews. Esther is the one who counters the threat and overcomes it by her subtlety and wisdom. It could be that the narrator loses some interest once the tension-filled parts of the story are over; it is true that the characters of Esther and Mordecai are presented as stereotypes in Chapters 8 and 9 and without much liveliness. Only the king steps out of his assigned role somewhat when, for once, he takes some initiative in approaching Esther (9:12). It is the king to whom the story turns in its final words:

1. Now King Ahasuerus laid a tax on the land and on the islands. 2. And all his achievements and his might and the full account of the greatness of Mordecai, whom the king had made great, are these not written in the book of the daily records of the kings of Media and Persia? 3. For Mordecai, the Jew, was second to King Ahasuerus and great among the Jews and liked by his many brothers, pursuing the good of his people and speaking peace to all his descendants.

As others have observed, these verses are not satisfactory and wrap nothing up; they almost sound like the beginning of a new story. What is the significance of the mention of a tax? Is a tax considered an accomplishment? Is this entire section a tip of the hat to the foreign power that had dominion over the Jews both inside and outside Judah at the time the story was told? Even for taxes one feigns gratitude in this context? Finally, the allusion to the king's many achievements and Mordecai's basking in the sunshine of his monarch, with Esther gone from the scene, is perhaps not how we would have ended the story. We may consider such a ragged ending to our advantage, however, as we consider that life rarely has tidy endings and that in this sense the Book of Esther is true to real life as it is lived messily with loose ends and threads coming undone. Esther is a story, after all, that has its setting in real life, the life of the Jews in Persia, the life of the Jews in the Diaspora, the life of the Jews with Christians and Christians with Jews. And the story is not over yet.

For Reflection and Discussion

1. I have compared Esther to a Br'er Rabbit story. Are you familiar with these stories? What is their setting? Read a Br'er Rabbit story with your study group. Can you identify analogies to Esther? Can you find an Esther, a Mordecai, or a King Ahasuerus in the stories?

2. The last time that Esther intercedes for her people (8:3-6), she is portrayed as weeping. Discuss the role of tears in women's lives. How do tears make you feel? How do others in your environment experience your tears? Describe different kinds of tears. Is the portrayal of Esther here more realistic or less so than before? Is she in character at this point in the story?

3. Think of a difficult task that you and/or your community had to accomplish that became wearisome and on which you burned out. What most made it difficult? Describe concretely the difficulties of the task itself and possible obstructions that had to be met and overcome.

4. I mention the funny side of the reversal in the roles of people and communities as well as the negative side. The modern nation of Israel was born in a context of persecution and attempts to annihilate all the Jews. The violence that we witness in this nation is a continuation of the violence perpetrated on the Jews across the ages, but especially during the Second World War. This recognition does not mean we condone blindly everything the State of Israel does, but it does mean we take seriously a Christian need for repentance and understanding that must preface any statement about Israel and the Jews from the side of the church. Discuss the implications of this statement.

5. Reversals of victims and victimizers are sometimes seen as unavoidable. What motivates groups who were formerly victimized to exercise victimization? How does this work in the legal system with capital punishment, for example? What are problems with this process? What is the formal position of your denomination on the death penalty? What is the law in your state?

6. Jews are generally sensitive when outsiders criticize the policies of the State of Israel. They suspect that the criticism hides anti-Jewishness. Moreover, they charge that critics apply standards for judging Israel that they do not apply to other nation states. Is there truth in these charges? How can we affirm that Jews are entitled to a Jewish state and homeland while also affirming the rights of Palestinian people? What is our responsibility for peace in the Middle East and in the world as American citizens and Christians? Could you begin conversation in your community among Jews, Christians, Moslems, and people of other faiths that are represented on sensitive issues of difference?

7. Are you acquainted with Purim and its customs? You may want to

invite someone from a local synagogue to help you with information and insight into the significance of this festival for the Jews. Are there special foods associated with Purim?

8. Read Judges 4:17-22. Is it more troubling to read about violence perpetrated by women than by men, even if it is for a just cause? Use my book *Reformed and Feminist—A Challenge to the Church* (Westminster John Knox, 1991) as a resource (pages 70-77).

9. Discuss the way Esther and Mordecai move in and out of the story in the last chapters. Could there be a deliberate effort at work here to put Esther's role in the shadow? Which character is most vivid in your recollection for the way you learned the story in the tradition of your faith community? Is Mordecai most "real" to you? At what moment in the story do you best remember him? Stories are always told from a certain point of interest or bias. Recalling for ourselves what we remember and who we remember from a story may help us to discover our own interests as well as that of the storytellers.

Prayer

God our shepherd who watches over us like a father, who guides and nurtures us like a mother, we give you thanks for the company of Esther and Vashti, Naomi and Ruth, in whose presence we have walked. Teach us to gather both wits and energy, imagination and love, to strive for the well-being of your creation, the work of your loving hands; to care for those who are helpless; to bring about just laws that may ease the hunger, disease, and deprivation in our land and in all the world; to love and tend our mother the earth and the human community with compassion and devotion. Give us zeal for the work of justice and love in creation. Make us so able through the power of your Spirit. Amen.

RESOURCES

RUTH

Compromising Redemption: Relating Characters in the Book of Ruth, by Danna N. Fewell and David M. Gunn (Literary Currents in Biblical Interpretation, Westminster John Knox Press, 1990)

Ezra, Nehemiah, and Esther, by Johanna W. H.van Wijk-Bos (The Westminster Bible Companion series, edited by Patrick D. Miller and David L.Bartlett; Westminster John Knox Press, 1998)

God and the Rhetoric of Human Sexuality, by Phyllis Trible (Fortress, 1978)

Reformed and Feminist—A Challenge to the Church, by Johanna W. H.van Wijk-Bos (Westminster John Knox Press, 1991)

Ruth, by Edward F. Campbell (Anchor Bible, Doubleday & Co., 1975)

Ruth in Berit Olam—Studies in Hebrew Narrative and Poetry, by Tod Linafelt, edited by David W. Cotter, Jerome T. Walsh, and Chris Franke (Collegeville, Minnesota, 1999)

The New Interpreter's Bible, Vol. II (Abingdon, 1998)

ESTHER

Esther, by Carey A. Moore (Anchor Bible, Doubleday & Co., 1977)

Esther in Berit Olam—Studies in Hebrew Narrative and Poetry, by Timothy K. Beal, edited by David W. Cotter, Jerome T. Walsh, and Chris Franke (Collegeville, Minnesota, 1999)

Ezra, Nehemiah, and Esther, by Johanna W.H.van Wijk-Bos (The Westminster Bible Companion series, edited by Patrick D. Miller and David L. Bartlett (Westminster, 1998)

The New Interpreter's Bible, Vol. III (Abingdon, 1999)

GENERAL RESOURCES

The Ancient Near East in Pictures Relating to the Old Testament, edited by James B. Pritchard (Princeton University Press, 1954)

Discovering Eve: Ancient Israelite Women in Context, by Carol Meyers (Oxford University Press, 1988)

Helpmates, Harlots and Heroes—Women's Stories in the Hebrew Bible, by Alice Ogden Bellis (Westminster John Knox, 1994)

A History of Israel, by John Bright (Westminster, 1981)

The Oxford Bible Atlas, edited by Herbert G. May (Oxford University Press, 1981)

Reformed and Feminist—A Challenge to the Church, by Johanna W. H.van Wijk-Bos (Westminster John Knox, 1991)

Reformed Theology and the Jewish People, edited by Alan P. F. Sell, (The World Alliance of Reformed Churches, 1986)

Reimagining God—A Case for Scriptural Diversity, by Johanna W. H.van Wijk-Bos (Westminster John Knox, 1995)

Religion and Sexism, edited by Rosemary Radford Ruether (Simon and Schuster, 1974)